Ten Tales
from
Dumfries &
Galloway

Ten Tales

from

Dumfries & Galloway

DAVID CARROLL

The
History
Press

For Betty Walsh – at ninety

First published 2010
Reprinted 2012

The History Press
The Mill, Brimscombe Port
Stroud, Gloucestershire, GL5 2QG
www.thehistorypress.co.uk

British Library Cataloguing in Publication Data.
A catalogue record for this book is available from the British Library.

ISBN 978 0 7509 4419 9

Typesetting and origination by The History Press
Printed in Great Britain

CONTENTS

ACKNOWLEDGEMENTS

I am grateful to David Higham Associates, for permission to quote an extract from *Five Red Herrings* by Dorothy L. Sayers (New English Library edition). Every reasonable effort has been made to contact copyright holders where this has been appropriate. I apologize for any unintentional omissions, and I would be pleased to rectify them (upon notification) in any subsequent edition of this work. I am grateful to Matilda Richards at The History Press for steering me through this project, and to Bernadette Walsh for her invaluable technical support. All photographs were taken by the author.

INTRODUCTION

S cratch the surface of any village, town, county or region in the British Isles, and you will almost certainly be rewarded with a rich seam of historical interest. That is certainly the case in Dumfries and Galloway, a vast tract of south-west Scotland embracing the old and much-cherished counties of Dumfriesshire, Wigtownshire and the Stewartry of Kirkcudbright. Somewhat underestimated, I often feel, by those people who are not acquainted with its delights at first hand, Dumfries and Galloway boasts forests, moorland, mountains and a magnificent coastline and is one of Britain's great national and natural treasures.

In the ten chapters that comprise this modest book, I have selected some of those people, places and events which – in their various ways – made a particular impression on me when first I came to live in this region a quarter of a century ago. (A different writer, tackling the same theme, might well have chosen to include subjects that I have omitted, and vice versa.)

For example, it is a source of constant amazement to me that such a thinly populated region (a fairly recent statistic placed the number of people per square mile at around only sixty) could have produced or have such close connections with characters so rich and varied as Henry Duncan, 'Founder of the Savings Banks', and John Paul Jones, 'Father of the American Navy'; or with Scotland's national bard, Robert Burns, and Thomas Carlyle the 'Sage of Chelsea'.

Equally varied are some of Dumfries and Galloway's more notable towns and villages: Moffat, for example, has a lucrative history as an elegant spa resort; Wanlockhead is not only Scotland's highest village, but is also famous for its lead and gold deposits; and Kirkcudbright, towards the close of the nineteenth and well into the twentieth century, proved a magnet for some of the country's finest and most famous artists.

The largely unsung heroism of two nineteenth-century mail-coach men is also recalled here, and we follow their ultimately tragic struggle in the line of duty, played out in severe blizzards and freezing temperatures beyond the Devil's Beef Tub, high above Moffat. The sombre theme continues with the final chapter and its account of the Quintinshill rail crash in May 1915, which remains to this day Britain's worst ever railway disaster.

I hope these brief glimpses into Dumfries and Galloway's diverse and rich past will give the reader as much pleasure as they have afforded me in the researching and writing of them.

David Carroll, Shieldhill, 2009

✣ ONE ✣

'JEANIE DEANS':
THE STORY OF HELEN WALKER

When Helen Walker died in 1791, at her humble and long-since demolished cottage known as 'Knowehead' (at Cluden in the parish of Irongray, a short distance north-west of Dumfries) she was buried in an unmarked grave in the secluded local churchyard. It seemed an entirely fitting end to her retiring and outwardly uneventful life.

Helen was the daughter of an agricultural labourer, after whose death she lived with her widowed mother and younger sister Isobel. We are able to catch a glimpse of her through the writing of John M'Diarmid who, in his *Sketches from Nature* (1830), recorded the impressions of Elizabeth Grierson who, when a girl, 'sixty years since', had known Helen well:

> Her conversational powers were of a high order, considering her humble situation in life … her language most correct, ornate and pointed; her deportment sedate and dignified in the extreme. Many of the neighbours regarded her as a 'little pensy body' – that is, conceited or proud; but at the same time they bore willing testimony to her exemplary conduct and unwearied attendance on the duties of religion. Wet or dry she appeared regularly at the parish church, and even when at home delighted in searching the Scriptures daily … On one occasion, [Helen] told Elizabeth Grierson that she should not do as she had done, but 'winnow the corn when the wind blew in the barn-door'. By this she meant that she should not hold her head too high, by rejecting the offer of a husband when it came in her way. [Helen herself remained unmarried throughout her life].

Helen largely succeeded in making ends meet by rearing chickens, working in the fields and, during the winter months, 'footing' stockings, '… an operation which bears the same relation to the hosier's craft that the cobbler's does to the shoemaker's', explained M'Diarmid. 'It has been reported too,' he added, 'that she sometimes taught children to read, but as no one [in the area] remembers this fact, I am inclined to regard it as somewhat apocryphal.'

The Heart of Midlothian, set into the cobbles of Parliament Square, Edinburgh, marks the site of the gallows (where convicted prisoners were hanged) outside the now-demolished Tolbooth prison.

Helen's life proved to be long, respectable and apparently quite ordinary, but there lurked an incident in her far-distant past which, long after her own death, would transform her – in the world's eyes, at least – from plain Helen Walker into the fictional 'Jeanie Deans', the heroine of Sir Walter Scott's *The Heart of Midlothian*, which was first published in 1818. Scott's novels, of course, enjoyed the level of popularity during his lifetime, and in the years following his death, that most authors can only dream about, with the appearance of each new work being an eagerly anticipated event. He made his mark originally as a compiler of traditional ballads, with the three-volume *Minstrelsy of the Scottish Border* (1802-3), after which there came a number of major original poetical works, including 'Marmion' (1808) and 'The Lady of the Lake' (1810). *Waverley*, the first of his many novels, appeared in 1814, and these continued in a stream of at least one a year until shortly before his death in 1832. *Waverley* and its successors were originally published anonymously, with Scott not acknowledging the authorship of his novels until as late as 1827.

The title of *The Heart of Midlothian* derived from the ironic name that was bestowed on Edinburgh's prison, the Tolbooth; a building which provides the focal point for the two loosely interconnecting plots of Scott's novel: the city's Porteous Riots of 1736 (which reached their climax with the hanging of the Captain of Edinburgh's Town Guard, John Porteous, by an angry mob), and the trial for child murder of 'Effie

Deans'. Both plots were closely based on real-life incidents, although inevitably Scott employed a degree of poetic licence in each case, especially when dealing with the distressing trial of the accused young mother.

Helen Walker was twenty-seven when, in May 1738, her sister Isobel was found guilty of child murder. The trial, which took place more than eighteen months after the sad event, was held at the High Court in Dumfries, housed in the town's distinctive Midsteeple building. M'Diarmid explained that:

> [Isobel], courted by a youth of the name of Waugh, who had the character of being rather wild, fell a victim to his snares, and became enceinte [i.e. pregnant], though she obstinately denied the fact to the last. The neighbours, however, suspected that a child had been born, and repeatedly urged her to confess her fault. But she was deaf to their entreaties, and denied all knowledge of a dead infant which was found shortly after in the Cairn, or Clouden [*sic*].

It was the opinion of the counsel for the defence that a word from Helen, testifying that her sister had, in fact, confided in her about the infant's birth, might well secure Isobel's release, but as this had not been the case, the devoutly religious Helen felt unable to speak it. Although the two sisters were very close, Helen steadfastly refused to commit perjury in order to save Isobel's life, saying that irrespective of the trial's outcome she must obey her conscience when giving evidence under oath in the witness-box. Isobel was duly convicted of child murder and sentenced to be hanged six weeks later. Her plight was mirrored by 'Effie Deans'. Addressing her in *The Heart of Midlothian*, the Judge declared:

> It is my painful duty to tell you that your life is forfeited under a law, which, if it may seem in some degree severe, is yet wisely so, to render those of your unhappy situation aware what risk they run, by concealing, out of pride or false shame, their lapse from virtue, and making no preparation to save the lives of the unfortunate infants they are to bring into the world.

However, Helen Walker's refusal to give a false testimony at Isobel's trial did not mean that she was averse to taking other steps (literally so, in her case) in order to save her sister's life, if that were still possible. On the same day that Isobel was convicted, Helen enlisted the help of a clerk at the court to draw up a petition which she could take in person to London, in the somewhat forlorn hope of obtaining the King's Pardon. That evening she set off alone to make the entire journey of over 300 miles from Dumfries to the capital on foot; this was an enterprise which, as M'Diarmid pointed out, 'was then considered more formidable than a voyage to America is in our day.' In *The Heart of Midlothian*, Helen's fictional counterpart set off south from Edinburgh:

The Midsteeple, Dumfries, where Isobel Walker was tried for child murder, and found guilty, in May 1738.

… using the mode of conveyance with which nature had provided [her] … With a strong heart and a frame patient of fatigue, Jeanie Deans, travelling at the rate of twenty miles a-day, and sometimes farther, traversed the southern part of Scotland, and advanced as far as Durham … Hitherto she had been either among her own country-folk, or those to whom bare feet and tartan … were objects too familiar to attract much attention. But as she advanced, she perceived that both circumstances exposed her to sarcasm and taunts, which she might otherwise have escaped … At York, our pilgrim stopped for the best part of a day – partly to recruit her strength – partly because she had the good luck to obtain a lodging in an inn kept by a countrywoman.

Finally, at Stamford, Jeanie (unlike Helen) '… obtained a place in the coach, which, although termed a light one, and accommodated with no fewer than six horses, only reached London on the afternoon of the second day.'

Taking up Helen's own story, M'Diarmid explained how:

… over her best attire she threw a plaid and hood … and completed the distance in fourteen days. Though her feet were sorely blistered, her whole frame exhausted, and her spirits sadly jaded, she found it impossible to rest until she had inquired her way to the residence of John, Duke of Argyle [who, she had been informed, would be best placed to act on her behalf in the matter of obtaining a Royal Pardon]. As she arrived at the door, his Grace was just about to step into his carriage, and as the moment was too crucial to be lost, the heroic pilgrim presented her petition, fell upon her knees, and urged its prayers with a degree of earnestness and natural elegance, that more than realized the well-known saying of 'snatching a grace beyond the reach of art' ... The Pardon was procured and despatched to Scotland, and the pilgrim, after her purse had been replenished, returned home, gladdened and supported by the consoling thought that she had done her duty without violating her conscience.

By the time Helen arrived back in Dumfriesshire, having saved her sister from the gallows, she had walked the astonishing distance of almost 700 miles in little more than a month.

Subsequently, Isobel married the father of her dead child, spending a long – and, it is believed – happy life at Whitehaven in Cumberland. The two sisters wrote to each other regularly until Helen's death, and it was Isobel's habit to send up to Irongray once a year a cheese and 'pepper-cake', 'portions of which [Helen] took great pleasure in presenting to her friends and neighbours.'

As for Helen, she returned to her peaceful and anonymous life at Irongray; a life, as M'Diarmid expressed it, of 'quiet rural employments and ... unsullied integrity.' She did not discuss with any of her neighbours the incident which would one day make her name well-known around the world, but she nevertheless became much respected among those people in her local community who knew about the selfless act of devotion she performed on behalf of her sister.

That, quite simply, might have been the end of Helen Walker's story (and one of which the world would have remained in ignorance), had it not been for the fact that in the year prior to Helen's death at the age of eighty, Mrs Helen Goldie, wife of the Commissary of Dumfries, Thomas Goldie, had taken a cottage for the summer near the remains of Lincluden Abbey, the twelfth-century convent for Benedictine nuns which Burns famously eulogised as:

> ... yon roofless tower,
> Where the wa'flow'r scents the dewy air,
> Where the houlet mourns in her ivy bower,
> And tells the midnight moon her care ...

Helen also lived close to this once-romantic spot and, hearing one day that her elderly neighbour sold chickens, Mrs Goldie went to buy some from her. The two women fell into conversation, and, before they parted, Mrs Goldie asked the name of her new acquaintance, whose commonsense and intelligence had made such a favourable impression on her. 'My name,' replied the elderly neighbour, 'is Helen Walker, but your husband kens weel about me.'

Mrs Goldie was due to leave the area the next day, and she did not return until the following spring. In the meantime, however, she had learned something of Helen

Remains of the twelfth-century Lincluden Abbey.

Walker's fascinating history from her husband the Commissary, and decided to visit the old woman again when she returned to the cottage near Lincluden Abbey. Sadly, though, Helen had died in her absence.

Mrs Goldie wrote an account of her meeting with Helen Walker, setting down her personal impressions together with as many details of Helen's story as she had gleaned from her husband. She sent these recollections anonymously to Sir Walter Scott, a quarter-of-a-century after Helen's death, stating that:

> I endeavoured to obtain some account of Helen from an old woman who inhabited the other end of her cottage … I enquired if Helen ever spoke of her past history, her journey to London &c. 'Na,' the old woman said, 'Helen was a wily body, and whene'er ony o' the neebors asked anything about it, she aye turned the conversation.' In short, every answer I received only tended to increase my regret, and raise my opinion of Helen Walker, who could unite so much prudence with so much heroic virtue.

Mrs Goldie also told Scott that she '… once proposed that a small monument should have been erected [in the churchyard at Irongray] to commemorate so remarkable a character, but I now prefer leaving it to you to perpetuate her memory in a more durable manner.' (At that time, her resting-place in the churchyard could only be identified by 'a stane taken off the dyke'.) Later, after Mrs Goldie herself had died, her daughter wrote to Scott confirming that her mother had:

… endeavoured to collect further particulars of Helen Walker, particularly concerning her journey to London, but found this nearly impossible; as the natural dignity of her character, and a high sense of family respectability, made her so indissolubly connect her sister's disgrace with her own exertions, that none of her neighbours durst ever question her upon the subject.

Nevertheless, we are indebted to Mrs Goldie's account for another fleeting visual impression of Helen Walker, captured on this occasion during the last year of her long life. The Commissary's wife described her as 'rather stout-looking … she was almost covered with a tartan plaid, and her cap had over it a black silk hood, tied under the chin – a piece of dress still much in use among elderly women of that rank of life in Scotland. Her eyes were dark and remarkably lively and intelligent.'

Having been sufficiently impressed by the story of Helen's epic journey and its purpose, to weave a similar incident into *The Heart of Midlothian* Scott, writing (in 1830) in the Introduction to a later edition of his novel, declared himself obliged …

> … to [Mrs Goldie] who thus supplied him with a theme affording such a pleasing view of the moral dignity of virtue, though unaided by birth, beauty or talent. If the picture has suffered in the execution … it is the failing of the author's powers to present in detail the same simple and striking portrait, exhibited in Mrs Goldie's letter.

'Jeanie Deans' was to become Scott's personal favourite among all the heroines he created, claiming that 'the lass kept tugging at my heart-strings'. Isobel, as we have seen, also appears in the tale, as 'Effie Deans'.

According to Miss Goldie, it remained her mother's dearest wish until the end of her life to have a tombstone placed over Helen Walker's grave with an inscription on it written by 'the Wizard of the North'. Scott responded more than favourably to the idea, writing in March 1830 to the local minister of Kirkpatrick-Irongray, the Revd David Dow, requesting permission '… to erect a simple monument … to a poor woman of the name of Walker respectable in her time for an act of great worth and fortitude.' The words he composed, inscribed on the memorial which he paid for out of his own pocket, can still be read on the stone tablet today:

> This stone was erected by the author of 'Waverley' to the memory of Helen Walker, who died in the year of God 1791. This humble individual practised in real life the virtues with which fiction has invested the imaginary character of 'Jeanie Deans': refusing the slightest departure from veracity, even to save the life of a sister, she nevertheless showed her kindness and fortitude in rescuing her from the severity of the Law, at the expense of personal exertions which the time rendered as difficult as the motive was laudable.

Over the ensuing years, as Helen Walker's fame spread and her connection with the character of 'Jeanie Deans' became more generally known, sightseers and souvenir-hunters simply ignored the heartfelt plea at the end of Scott's inscription, to 'respect the grave of poverty when combined with love of truth and dear affection.'

Helen Walker's tombstone, with its protective iron railings, in Irongray churchyard.

Fragments of the memorial began to disappear to such an extent – or, as J.M. Sloan, author of *The Carlyle Country*, pithily phrased it in 1904, 'the stone was getting its dimensions seriously abridged by pilfering visitors' – that, eventually, it became necessary to place an iron railing around the monument for its own protection.

One can only imagine the astonishment of self-effacing Helen Walker, could she but know how famous she has become, immortalised as the fictional heroine of what is still regarded today as one of Scott's finest novels. 'That a character so distinguished for her undaunted love of virtue, lived and died in poverty, if not want,' concluded Scott, 'serves only to show us how insignificant, in the sight of Heaven, are our principal objects of ambition upon earth.'

TWO

JOHN PAUL JONES: 'FATHER OF THE AMERICAN NAVY'

Largely because of its relatively sheltered and somewhat gentler climate, compared with other wilder and more exposed tracts of the region, Kirkbean – thirteen miles or so south-east of Dumfries – and the area surrounding it, is sometimes referred to (perhaps a touch optimistically) as the 'Garden of Galloway'. Resting below the imposing height of Criffel which – rising to an altitude of 1,800ft and towering over the surrounding countryside – is easily recognisable for miles around, the village sits inland a mile or so from Carsethorn, the place at which the River Nith flows into the Solway Firth. Once a thriving outport, serving Dumfries during the eighteenth century, Carsethorn was the last point of contact with their native land for many thousands of Scots who were driven by hardship and poverty to seek a new way of life across the Atlantic, or on the other side of the world in Australia, during the late eighteenth and early nineteenth century. It was here (and further upstream at Glencaple and Kingholm Quay) where vessels that were too large to navigate the Nith as far as Dumfries were able to unload their cargoes for subsequent transportation by road.

Appropriately, perhaps, given its proximity to the coast, Kirkbean has nurtured two renowned seafaring men. The slightly earlier – and now less famous – of the pair was Admiral John Campbell. He was born the son of the local minister of the village around 1720 and, in the early days of his career, between 1740 and 1744, he circumnavigated the globe under the supervision of the English naval commander, George Anson. He became a noted pioneer in the field of naval navigation and, in 1782, towards the end of his life, he was made Commander-in-Chief and Governor of Newfoundland.

Meanwhile, three years after Campbell had completed his voyage around the world, the head gardener's wife on Kirkbean's local Arbigland Estate gave birth to a son in the small stone cottage that was the family's tied home. The boy was called John Paul, (only adding 'Jones' to his name during the 1770s in an attempt, it is said, to conceal his true identity after killing a sailor in self-defence).

The remains of the old jetty at Carsethorn, from where many thousands of emigrants left Scotland for ever.

The owner of Arbigland at the time of John Paul's birth was William Craik, now generally regarded as quite an enlightened agriculturalist in his day, who became the first President of the Society for the Improvement of Agriculture in south-west Scotland.

From the outset, it seemed that John Paul's life would in some way be devoted to the sea. James Craik, who was also born at Arbigland and eventually became George Washington's personal physician, explained that the young lad '… would run to Carsethorn whenever his father would let him off, talk to the sailors and clamber over the ships,' adding that 'he taught his playmates to manoeuvre their little boats to mimic a naval battle, while, taking his stand on the tiny cliff overlooking the roadstead, shouted shrill commands to his imaginary fleet.'

In 1761, when still only thirteen years of age, John Paul left school and sailed from Carsethorn over to Whitehaven on the Cumberland coast, from where he began his life at sea as a lowly ship's boy. His earliest voyages, on the Whitehaven-based vessel *Friendship*, whisked him across the Atlantic to Virginia, where he was able to make contact with his tailor brother, William, who had emigrated to America and settled in Fredericksburg.

As the years unfolded, John Paul sailed aboard a variety of different vessels and rose through the ranks with commendable speed. Good fortune smiled on him, at least, (if not on others) when – in 1768 – the captain of the ship on which John Paul was sailing at that time died while still at sea, and the twenty-one-year-old young man from Kirkbean was subsequently made master of the vessel.

After leading voyages to the Indies and elsewhere over the ensuing few years, John Paul (having added 'Jones' to his name at this time) gravitated to America during the

John Paul Jones's birthplace and childhood home.

early 1770s, where he began his association with that country's naval service which was then in its infancy. In 1775 the American War of Independence began and it would continue to rage for eight years. Jones's sympathies lay with the colonists, and thus he was to come into direct contact with the fleet of the British Navy.

Three well-documented incidents in particular stand out from those turbulent years. In the spring of 1778, while sailing aboard the American sloop *Ranger*, Jones made his way northwards up the Irish Sea. He went ashore at his old port of Whitehaven with a party of his men, intent on disabling the forts that protected the harbour. However, although he achieved his objective, the whole enterprise ended somewhat unsatisfactorily, one suspects, from Jones's point of view, owing to some disobedience and no small amount of drunkenness among his crew. He did not leave the seaport town (where his own naval career had begun many years earlier), though, without first setting light to a vessel or two in Whitehaven harbour. One can only imagine the feelings of the local population, for their town to have been on the receiving end of such treatment from a man who had been born and brought up so close to them, on the other side of the Solway.

However, the firing of Whitehaven harbour, as this incident has since become known, was not to be the end of that night's work for the men of the sloop *Ranger*. A further few hours' sailing brought Jones and his crew to the Solway coast off Kirkcudbright where, at St Mary's Isle in Kirkcudbright Bay, during the morning of the next day, Jones intended to seize the Earl of Selkirk at his home, and employ him as a bargaining counter for the release of imprisoned American seamen. However, Jones found that the earl was away from home and only the countess was in attendance. Not daunted, the crew of the *Ranger* – denied the pleasure of taking the earl himself – were determined to make their unheralded visit worthwhile, and contented themselves with removing the family's silverware.

Perhaps his own local connections and dormant loyalties weighed heavily on that occasion, because Jones subsequently regretted the fact that he had allowed his men to carry off the Selkirk plate. He gave back to the earl every item that had been removed from St Mary's Isle, once hostilities between Britain and America had ceased. Jones wrote to the earl in February 1784 stating that:

> The long delay that has happened to the restoration of your plate has given me much concern and I now feel a proportionate pleasure in fulfilling what was my first intention. My motive for landing at your estate in Scotland was to take you as an hostage for the lives and liberty of a number of the citizens of America, who had been taken in war on the ocean and committed to British prisons ... I am glad that you were absent from your estate when I landed there, as I bore no personal enmity, but the contrary towards you.

The third famous incident occurred during the autumn of 1779, when Jones was again sailing in British waters, on this occasion off the Yorkshire coast at Flamborough Head. He was in command of the vessel *Bonhomme Richard* when, during the night of 23 September, he went into battle against the two British warships, the sloop *Countess of Scarborough* and the frigate *Serapis*. The engagement proved to be a long and bloody affair. Many sailors, on both sides, were either terribly injured or lost their lives, and the *Bonhomme Richard* was eventually sunk. However, despite the loss of his own ship, together with many of his men, Jones himself survived and was even able to take as his prisoner Captain Pearson of the *Serapis*, aboard which ailing vessel he retreated to Holland.

In his subsequent report of the battle, which he submitted to the Admiralty Office, Pearson wrote that:

> I found it in vain, and indeed impracticable from the situation we were in, to stand out any longer with the least prospect of success ... The first lieutenant and myself were immediately escorted into the ship alongside when we found her to be an American ship-of-war ... of 40 guns and 375 men, commanded by Capt. Paul Jones ... the *Bonhomme Richard* herself was in the greatest distress ... She also was on fire in two places, and 6 or 7ft of water in her hold, which kept increasing on them all night and the next day, til they were obliged to quit her, and she sunk with a great number of her wounded people on board her.

It is hardly surprising that these exploits caused Jones to be regarded as something of a pirate or renegade in his own country. Indeed, the nineteenth-century statesman and novelist, Benjamin Disraeli, wrote – perhaps with a hint of melodrama – that 'the nurses of Scotland hushed their crying charges with the whisper of his name.'

Jones subsequently went on to devote much of his time and energy to help formulate training and improve discipline in the young American navy – a campaign

Memorial cairn in the garden of Jones's cottage.

that, as Richard F. Bickford points out in *The Story of John Paul Jones* (1993), would eventually bear fruit with the founding of the Annapolis Naval College. The impact he made on the development of the service is also reflected in the sobriquet 'Father of the American Navy', by which he is widely known.

Jones served briefly in the Russian Navy towards the end of the 1780s, and was given the rank of Rear Admiral. However, by 1790 he had settled in Paris where he died two years later, but that was not quite the end of his story. Tom Watson, writing in the 1906 edition of William McDowall's *History of the Burgh of Dumfries* explained what happened next:

> The body was placed in a lead coffin, in spirits, and buried in St Louis Cemetery, the intention being that it should at some convenient season be taken to America. The convenient season did not come, because of devastating war in Europe and political and social upheaval. The cemetery was subsequently obliterated by a scheme of city improvements. But Paul never ceased to stir the imagination of American sailors … And six or seven years ago … the American Ambassador to France instituted a systematic

search for the long-forgotten grave … and in April of last year a coffin was unearthed containing a body in good preservation, which was identified as that of the adventurous sailor. It had been immersed in alcohol and packed with hay and straw … The body was conveyed to America on board a United States war vessel and temporarily buried there, awaiting the erection of a suitable mausoleum at Annapolis, Maryland.

An inscription on a plaque in the garden of Jones's cottage birthplace, presented by the Bath Iron Works Corporation of Maine, and mounted on a stone cairn flanked by the Scottish and American flags, completes the tale. 'He fought long and valiantly and successfully for the freedom of the American Colonies,' it proclaims, adding that Jones's remains 'were placed in the crypt of the U.S. Naval Academy Chapel, as an inspiration to our young naval leaders of the future.'

The birthplace of the 'Father of the American Navy' was officially opened to the public in 1993, after the cottage and its grounds had been gifted by the Trustees of Arbigland. (Check local details for opening times.) Attractively tucked away in secluded country close to the water's edge, beyond a network of narrow but well-signposted lanes, the small museum complex (which inevitably attracts many visitors from the United States every summer), includes a shop-cum-exhibition area housed in a building that was originally a cowshed and then served later as a gamekeeper's cottage. The room is furnished with illustrated panels documenting Jones's life and achievements, and contains a bronze bust executed in 1780 by the French classical sculptor, Jean-Antoine Houdon. Replicas of ships' flags and copies of contemporary press reports recounting Jones's various exploits adorn the walls, and an illuminating audio-visual presentation helps to bring Jones's colourful personality to life for visitors.

A few steps away, across a neatly kept lawn, stands the traditional whitewashed John Paul Jones Cottage. The interior of the building, with its low-beamed ceiling and stone-flagged floor, has been expertly recreated to reflect the mid-eighteenth-century style that was common in homes of this kind at the time of Jones's childhood. A steep wooden staircase reaches up to a loft where the children of the family slept and, on the ground floor, the area is divided by a wooden partition into a general living area and the parents' bedroom. There is a large open fireplace at either end (the living room hearth is dotted about with stone pots and iron cooking utensils), and the place is simply furnished with low chairs and a high-backed settle, together with a cot and curtained cabinet-bed, all fashioned from sturdy wood. No doubt, were Jones able to step back into his old home today, he would be startled – and perhaps pleased – to discover that an additional room had been built to represent the cabin of his ship *Bonhomme Richard*. But there could hardly be a greater contrast than between the remote and homely cottage at the edge of the Solway where Jones spent his country childhood, and the third-floor apartment in Paris where he ended his days during the summer of 1792, dying less than a fortnight after his forty-fifth birthday.

Above & below: *The recreated interior of Jones's childhood home.*

THE LAST YEARS
OF ROBERT BURNS

R obert Burns was thirty years of age, and had barely seven years to live, when he
settled in Dumfriesshire during the summer of 1789, at Ellisland Farm about
six miles north-west of Dumfries and close beside the River Nith. Burns leased
the 170-acre farm from Patrick Miller, who owned the Dalswinton estate (of which
Ellisland formed a part), and who had become acquainted with Burns when the poet
was staying in Edinburgh during 1786. Miller, incidentally, is an interesting character
in his own right. In October 1788, a steamboat pioneered by him was launched on
Dalswinton Loch, and it has long been wondered whether Burns was one of the
passengers aboard the vessel on that historic day. Tradition asserts that he was, but Burns
himself seems never to have mentioned the incident in his work or correspondence.
Yet, as James A. Mackay observes in his incomparable *Burns-Lore of Dumfries and
Galloway* (1988), given that the poet was at Ellisland on the day in question, 'it seems
plausible that [he] would have taken an hour from his harvesting … to see an event
which must have been the talk of that quiet countryside.'

Ellisland was badly run-down when Burns came into possession of it, but he
was provided with £300 to build a farmhouse and erect fencing on his land.
In the event, the house-building proved to be such a long-winded affair that,
although Burns had signed the lease for the property in March 1788 (and had
begun working on the farm in June of that year), he did not actually move into
the farmhouse with his newly-wedded wife, Jean Armour, and their children until
the summer of 1789.

❧ ❧ ❧

Burns was born in January 1759 in a long low cottage ('the auld clay biggin') with
a thatched roof at Alloway, then a rural village but now on the southern fringe of
Ayr. At the age of seven, he moved with his family to Mount Oliphant, a farm to the
south-east of Alloway. The poet's brother, Gilbert, wrote later that:

Ellisland Farm, where Burns and his family lived from 1789-1791.

At the age of thirteen [Robert] assisted in threshing the crop of corn, and at fifteen was the principal labourer of the farm … I doubt not but the hard labour of this period of his life was in great measure the cause of that depression of spirits with which Robert was so often afflicted through the whole of his life afterwards.

During these early times, as Gilbert explained, 'the family … lived very sparingly. For several years butcher's meat was a stranger in the house, while all the members of the family exerted themselves to the utmost of their strength, and rather beyond it, in the labours of the farm.'

However, on a happier note, Burns composed his first known song while living at Mount Oliphant. In 1773, aged fourteen and inspired by Nelly Kilpatrick, a local blacksmith's daughter who was the boy's companion in the harvest field during that autumn, Burns wrote the words of 'Handsome Nell':

> O once I lov'd a bonie lass,
> Aye, and I love her still;
> And whilst that virtue warms my breast,
> I'll love my handsome Nell.

Recalling that time, ten years later, in his *First Commonplace Book*, he explained that:

I never had the least thought or inclination of turning poet till I once got heartily in love, and then rhyme and song were, in a manner, the spontaneous language of my heart.

[It] was the first of my performances. It is, indeed, very puerile and silly; but I am always pleased with it, as it recalls to my mind those happy days when my heart was yet honest, and my tongue was sincere.

Unable to make ends meet on the seventy-odd acres of Mount Oliphant, the family moved again in 1777 to Lochlea Farm, north-east of Tarbolton, where they stayed for seven years until the poet's father died in 1784. Later, Burns entered into a partnership with his brother at Mossgiel, near Mauchline, but the relentless hardship of farming in his native Ayrshire, coupled with a particularly turbulent period in his frequently complicated love-life, had made him consider seriously the possibility of emigrating to the West Indies. However, these plans were abandoned and, by the time Burns arrived at Ellisland Farm, he had already published the first – or Kilmarnock – edition of his *Poems, Chiefly in the Scottish Dialect* (1786), which had met with instant popular success. He had also been feted by Edinburgh's aristocracy and *literati* when staying in the Scottish capital.

Despite the celebrity that Burns's poems had brought him, and the success of what he himself described as his 'meteor appearance' among the great and the good of Edinburgh, the day-to-day reality of his life once he had settled down to work at Ellisland was a harsh one. Try as hard as he might, he could not make a success of the farm and, within only six months of settling his young family there, he took up a post as an exciseman at an annual salary of £50, in order to swell his income. By January 1790, he was telling Gilbert that, 'this farm has undone my enjoyment of myself. It is a ruinous affair on all hands. But let it go to hell!'

Although most of the poems for which Burns is best-remembered today, including 'The Holy Fair' and 'The Cottar's Saturday Night', had already appeared in his *Poems, Chiefly in the Scottish Dialect* by the time he arrived at Ellisland, it was here that he was to compose his last major poem, 'Tam o' Shanter', as visitors to present-day Ellisland will discover from a plaque fixed to a gate which leads to a wooded walk along the banks of the Nith. 'One autumn day in 1790', the plaque proclaims, 'Robert Burns paced up and down this grassy path crooning to himself in one of his poetical moods the words which became the immortal tale of "Tam o' Shanter". In the last field along the path the poet saw the wounded hare that inspired the "Address to a Wounded Hare".' 'Auld Lang Syne' was also a product of his days at Ellisland.

Although the nature of his work on the farm was arduous and unrewarding, there were compensations to be had for Burns in his life at Ellisland. A gregarious and charismatic man, Burns struck up a friendship with Captain Robert Riddell, owner of the neighbouring mansion, Friar's Carse, and its estate. Although they would eventually part on bad terms shortly before Riddell's death in 1794, Burns always retained fond memories of Friar's Carse and the family who lived there. 'At their fireside,' he wrote, 'I have enjoyed more pleasant evenings than at all the houses of fashionable people in this country put together; to their kindness and hospitality I am indebted for many of the happiest hours of my life.'

Captain Riddell built a small summerhouse, known as 'The Hermitage', in the grounds of his estate. It lay close to the boundary with Ellisland (indeed, it may still be seen today) and, as a trusted neighbour and guest, Burns was allowed to use it.

'The Hermitage', in the grounds of Friar's Carse Hotel. Burns spent many hours in this secluded summerhouse.

He inscribed the lines, beginning, 'Thou whom chance may hither lead / Be thou clad in russet weed ...' from his 'Verses in Friar's Carse Hermitage' (written in 1788) on a window-pane in the small building. The glass was later removed to the safety of Dumfries Museum.

One positive outcome resulting from Burns's friendship with Captain Riddell was the founding, in 1789, of the library of the Monkland Friendly Society in the village of Dunscore, to the west of Ellisland. The library operated at first from Monkland Cottage, but eventually moved to a house in the village's Main Street. Writing in 1791, Burns explained the purpose of the enterprise:

> To store the minds of the lower classes with useful knowledge is certainly of very great consequence, both to them as individuals and to society at large. Giving them a turn for reading and reflection is giving them a source of innocent and laudable amusement; and besides, raises them to a more dignified degree in the scale of rationality ...The plan [is] so simple as to be practicable in any corner of the country.

🐝 🐝 🐝

Burns left Ellisland during the autumn of 1791, thus finally bringing to a close his life on the land. He moved, with Jean and their children, into a tenement at the lower end of Bank Street, Dumfries, where they occupied just three rooms above the ground floor of the property. The building, as James A. Mackay relates, stood in what was then known officially as Cavarts or the Wee Vennel but which, for obvious reasons in that age of open sewers, had been dubbed locally the Stinking Vennel. (The property in question is still standing but privately owned, and is NOT open to the public.) The flat in Bank Street must have seemed rather cramped to Burns and his family after their larger house at Ellisland, with all the land surrounding it. A plaque, placed on the property in 1971, records the dates of Burns's occupation in what is described as the 'Songhouse of Scotland', and where the bard is said to have completed more than sixty poems and songs – including 'Ae Fond Kiss' and 'The Deil's Awa' wi' the Excise Man' – during his eighteen-months' residence.

The birth of another child in 1792 prompted a move to a more spacious home in Millbrae Vennel (later called Mill Street and now Burns Street) in May 1793. This would prove to be Burns's last home, where he would spend the remaining few years of his life.

Having given up farming, Burns was fully employed as an exciseman during the years he lived in Dumfries, and it was an occupation that gave him cause to travel extensively into the surrounding country. While living at Ellisland, his duties had taken him into the furthest reaches of Upper Nithsdale but, early in 1792, he was promoted to a post in the Dumfries Port Division. Ecclefechan, famously known as the birthplace of Thomas Carlyle, was one village that he visited occasionally and where, in February 1795 (the year of Carlyle's birth, incidentally), he was marooned in a heavy snowstorm. 'To add to my misfortune,' he wrote to a friend, 'since dinner a scraper has been torturing catgut in sounds that would have insulted the dying agonies of a sow under the hands of a butcher …' When passing through the mid-Annandale village of Lochmaben, in the course of his excise duties, Burns would stay at the manse as a guest of the local incumbent. Alluding to the fact that Lochmaben is set among a number of lochs, Burns referred to it as, 'Marjory o' the mony Lochs / A Carlin auld and teugh …' in one of his Election Ballads, 'The Five Carlins'.

Further south, where the River Sark flows into the Solway Firth just below Gretna, forming in the process part of the boundary between England and Scotland, Burns the exciseman took part in the capture of the smuggling vessel *Rosamond* at Sarkfoot in 1792, although there are varying accounts of his involvement in this incident. As a poet, however, he mentions the river in question in these famous lines:

> Now Sark rins over Solway sands,
> An' Tweed rins to the ocean,
> To mark where England's province stands –
> Such a parcel of rogues in a nation!

After the *Rosamond* had been seized by Burns and his fellow excisemen, it was taken for repairs to a boatyard at Kelton, a hamlet beside the River Nith a few miles south of Dumfries. Like his colleagues in the excise business, Burns was not immune from danger when carrying out his duties, as he discovered to his cost one day at Penpont,

Burns's House, Dumfries, where the poet spent the last few years of his life. It is now open to the public throughout the year.

near Thornhill, where he was set upon by a group of smugglers outside one of the village pubs.

Meanwhile, at home in Dumfries, Burns entered fully into the life of the town. Of course, these were the days of the French Revolutionary Wars and, on 26 March 1795, the poet assembled with his comrades at Dock Park for the first parade of the Royal Dumfries Volunteers. Apparently, the one hundred or so men who comprised the RDV were not required to march more than five miles from the centre of the town, inspiring Burns to offer the following toast at a Volunteers' dinner: 'May we never see the French, nor the French see us.' A few months after their formation, the RDV paraded into Queensberry Square to receive their colours in the shadow of the Queensberry Monument, before dining together at the King's Arms. No doubt this gave Burns the opportunity to recite his highly popular ballad, 'Does Haughty Gaul Invasion Threat?' (sometimes called 'The Dumfries Volunteers') which had first appeared in the *Dumfries Journal* in May of that year:

> Does haughty Gaul invasion threat?
> Then let the louns beware, sir:
> There's wooden walls upon our seas,
> And Volunteers on shore Sir …

The RDV was an earlier incarnation of – and in the same honourable tradition as – the Second World War's Home Guard, depicted so amusingly in the long-running BBC TV series *Dad's Army*. One can rest assured, however, that Burns would have been the antithesis of the dour, curmudgeonly Scot, Private Frazer, portrayed so admirably by that famous son of Dumfries, John Laurie.

Burns's gregarious nature inevitably made him a familiar figure in many of the Dumfries pubs of the day, but his spirit probably resides most potently in the place he called his 'favourite howff', the Globe Inn, tucked away in a close off the town's High Street and – established in 1610 and still thriving today – probably one of Scotland's oldest hostelries. He was a frequent visitor here not only when resident in Dumfries but also while he was living at Ellisland. There are many items on display at the Globe relating to the poet, and a Burns Room downstairs contains his chair and a collection of Burnsiana. Globe Inn Close itself was the subject of a restoration project during the Burns bicentenary year of 1996. Among various new installations marking Burns's connection with the Globe and its precincts, are several iron sculptures depicting scenes from 'Tam o' Shanter', and a block of red sandstone from the nearby quarry at Locharbriggs on which have been inscribed the opening lines from 'Ae Fond Kiss'.

Away from the cramped, smoke-filled bars of Dumfries, the banks of the River Nith provided Burns with one of his favourite haunts and, during the last few years of his life, he often wandered out of the town northwards to Lincluden, where he would sometimes linger among the remains of the Abbey, or he would saunter downstream to Castledykes, no doubt seeking inspiration as he went along. The Nith is a long river, rising near Cumnock and following a winding course for more than seventy miles before flowing into the Solway Firth. It became so much a part of Burns's life that he referred to it in more than one of his poems and songs. Perhaps he waxed most lyrically on the subject in 'The Banks of the Nith':

> How lovely, Nith, thy fruitful vales,
> Where bounding hawthorns gaily bloom;
> And sweetly spread thy sloping dales,
> Where lambkins wanton through the broom.
> Tho' wandering now must be my doom,
> Far from thy bonie banks and braes,
> May there my latest hours consume,
> Amang the friends of early days!'

(Burns Walk, along the banks of the Nith, is well-signposted today, allowing anyone with an interest in the poet literally to tread in his footsteps, although whether Burns himself would recognise the modern landscape is debatable.)

Burns's self-styled 'meteor appearance' in Edinburgh during the late-1780s contrasted sadly with his melancholy decline in Dumfries during the mid-1790s.

*The Globe Inn, Dumfries, was famously
described by Burns as his 'favourite howff'.*

Meteors have the invariable characteristic of burning out, and the long, hard years
of his farming life (not least at Ellisland, where he was not only running a farm
but sometimes also riding several hundred miles a week on excise duties over
the often arduous terrain of Upper Nithsdale), coupled with the demands of an
ever-expanding family and constant anxiety over money matters, produced the
inevitable detrimental effect on his health. At the close of 1795, he became very
ill with what was described as a 'most severe rheumatic fever'. As 1796 unfolded
Burns's decline continued, and during the first two weeks of July he took himself
off to the former hamlet of Brow, near Clarencefield, where he had been sent
by his physician to 'take the waters' of the chalybeate spring of Brow Well and
to swim in the nearby Solway Firth. The whole enterprise was almost certainly
ill-advised, and the weeks he passed at Brow Well did nothing to restore his health.
'I have been a week at sea-bathing,' Burns informed Gilbert, a week or two after
his arrival, 'and I will continue [here] or in a friend's house in the country all the
summer. God help my wife and children if I am taken from their head! They will
be poor indeed.' Burns returned to Dumfries on 18 July and died at home only
three days later of rheumatic heart disease.

Following his death, Burns's body was removed from the family home and taken
to the town's early eighteenth-century Midsteeple, where it lay in the courtroom
until the poet's funeral four days later. Burns and his family had attended worship at

The Grecian temple-style Burns's mausoleum in St Michael's churchyard, Dumfries.

St Michael's Church during their years in Dumfries (their box-pew has long since disappeared but a brass plate shows its position), and the poet's funeral service was conducted here, before his burial in the north-east corner of the churchyard. Burns's funeral was reputedly the largest occasion of its kind ever seen in Dumfries. Reports of the number of mourners who attended his remains through the town to his grave vary. The Dumfriesshire poet and man of letters, Allan Cunningham who, as a boy, walked in Burns's funeral procession, put the number at around 12,000, although this was an estimate he arrived at almost half a century later. 'Not a word was heard,' he recalled, 'and although all could not be near, and many could not see, when the earth closed on their darling poet for ever there was no rude impatience shewn.' On that same day Burns's newly-created widow, Jean, gave birth to their sixth child, a son who was named Maxwell.

In 1817, twenty-one years after his death, Burns's remains were transferred to a Grecian temple-style mausoleum, which was designed by Thomas Hunt and took two years to complete. Not only Burns himself, but also Jean and five members of their family, are entombed in the mausoleum which, as the poet's final resting-place, is an essential port of call for anyone following the town's 'Burns Trail'.

It is impossible to stray far in Dumfries without being reminded that Burns is intricately woven into the fabric of the place; the most visible confirmation of which

The Burns Statue, which has occupied a commanding position in the heart of Dumfries since 1882.

is possibly the Burns Statue, occupying a commanding position at the busy junction of High Street, Buccleuch Street and Church Crescent. Fashioned from Carrara marble and designed by Amelia Hill, the statue was financed by public subscription and unveiled in 1882. It has been slightly re-sited over the years to accommodate minor road alterations, but its dominant position is testimony to the special place that Burns occupies in the life and history of Dumfries. In addition, some of the town's oldest and most distinctive buildings have close associations with him; not only the Midsteeple, where his body lay in state before his funeral, or the 'Globe' where he spent so many convivial hours, but also the Theatre Royal in Shakespeare Street, for example, of which Burns was one of its earliest patrons, and the handsome red sandstone house in Burns Street where he spent his final days. Open to the public throughout the year, it contains books, letters, manuscripts and other material relating to his life and work, including the chair in which he wrote his last poems and the gun that he carried when on duty as an exciseman. Situated on the opposite side of the Nith, and housed in what was formerly the town's eighteenth-century corn mill at the river's edge, the Robert Burns Centre was opened in 1986 and includes a bookshop, café-gallery and audio-visual theatre (used as a cinema in the evenings), with displays and exhibitions relating to Burns's last years spent in the Dumfries of the 1790s, his own '... Maggy by the banks o' Nith / A dame wi' pride enough ...'

❧ FOUR ❧

THE REVD HENRY DUNCAN

Henry Duncan was born in 1774 at Lochrutton Manse, a few miles west of Dumfries. He came from a family of clergymen who, on his father's side, had been ministers of the parish of Lochrutton for several generations. On his mother's side, his great-grandfather, the Revd John MacMurdo of Torthorwald 'had been in the ministry so early as the beginning of [the eighteenth] century … [Duncan] could thus trace his descent on both sides, with little interruption, through a clerical ancestry, almost to the times of the Covenant; so numerous were his relations among the Scottish clergy, that he used to compare his family to the tribe of Levi …'

Given this impressive clerical pedigree, it was almost inevitable from his infancy that Henry Duncan would one day also enter the Church himself. For these details relating to his forbears, and for much of the information contained in this chapter about his life, we are indebted to a highly informative *Memoir* of Duncan written by his son – yet another clergyman – the Revd George Duncan, and published in 1848.

Henry Duncan was sent – with his younger brother, Thomas – to live with an aunt in Dumfries; where both boys attended the town's Academy, and where Henry distinguished himself as 'thoughtful and intelligent, fonder of reading than of play, and especially delighting in spirit-stirring narratives in rhyme or prose.' George Duncan goes on to explain how his father was:

> … described by one who knew him from early childhood, as a very engaging boy and a general favourite. With a fine clear but not florid complexion, an open ingenuous countenance, a profusion of golden curls, and an erect and manly air, his personal appearance was highly prepossessing; his mild and amiable manner, his sweet-tempered, kind and generous disposition, won for him a way to the good opinion and affectionate regard of all with whom he associated.

In 1788, Duncan attended St Andrew's University where, at the tender age of fourteen, he studied classics and logic. Two years later, however, he joined a firm of bankers in

Ruthwell Church, where Duncan began his ministry in 1799.

Liverpool through the influence of his relation James Currie, the Dumfriesshire-born physician and early editor and biographer of Robert Burns, who was practising in Liverpool at that time. However, it became increasingly evident from the outset that Duncan's heart was not in the banking profession. He wrote to his father in September 1793 saying:

> I feel within myself a great desire for knowledge, and in my idle hours am never happy unless engaged in some literary pursuit … As to my present situation, I have no actual dislike of it, but I do not feel interested enough in the business to derive any pleasure from it, and to discharge my duty as I ought to do. My disposition is entirely different from what a merchant's ought to be.

Duncan's father agreed that his son should change direction and, having just turned twenty, Henry began studying moral philosophy at Edinburgh University, under the guidance of the renowned Professor Dugald Stewart. He also spent some time at the University of Glasgow before returning home to Lochrutton in early 1798, when 'he was taken on trial for license by the Presbytery of Dumfries … the practical effect of [which] was to place him in circumstances for receiving, at some future period, a patron's presentation to a living …' Eighteen months or so later, as his son records, 'Duncan was ordained by the Presbytery of Annan to the pastoral charge of the parish of Ruthwell [on 19 September 1799], and was introduced to his flock on the following

Sabbath.' It must have proved a popular appointment from the beginning with the parishioners of that windswept Solway parish, because the 'sweet-tempered, kind and generous disposition' which had characterised Duncan as a child and in his youth were carried through to adulthood: 'the benevolence which always beamed from his open countenance', wrote his son, 'promised to his people that their intercourse would be distinguished, on his part, by the kindliest feelings.'

Duncan would stay at Ruthwell for well over forty years. When he arrived in the parish, however, he found matters in a state of some disarray. The previous incumbent had been ill for many years and, being unable to perform his duties, a series of temporary assistants had bridged the gap. His son wrote that:

> Mr Duncan found that the physical circumstances of his people were in many cases very distressing. Consecutive scanty harvests at the close of [the eighteenth] century had raised the price of provisions so extravagantly, that …it was impossible for the working classes to support nature …

No doubt here were sown the seeds in Henry Duncan's mind of what would, in due course, prove to be his most celebrated achievement: the founding of the savings banks movement.

In the meantime, the inhabitants of Ruthwell could count themselves fortunate in having acquired a minister such as Henry Duncan, because he was a talented man with a wide breadth of interests. For example, he was instrumental in founding a local newspaper, the *Dumfries and Galloway Courier*, whose first issue appeared on 6 December 1809. In his capacity as an amateur geologist, he made an important study of fossil footprints, working from a slab of red sandstone which had been recovered from the Corncockle Muir quarry near Templand, a few miles north-west of Lockerbie. Duncan's study generated wide-ranging debate and no small amount of controversy during the late-1820s, among some of the country's most eminent professional geologists; one of whom, Professor Buckland of Oxford, subsequently wrote to Duncan, telling him that, 'I look upon your discovery as one of the most curious and most important that has ever been made in geology … it is a discovery that will for ever connect your name with the progress of this science.' Obviously proud of his father's important contribution in the field of geology, George Duncan was at pains to stress in his *Memoir* that Henry Duncan's 'attention was first devoted to the subject while he was as yet but a tyro in the science, and that he had resolution, notwithstanding, to maintain and make out his case against the united authority of the whole race of contemporary geologists.'

However, Duncan is probably more widely known today for another remarkable discovery, and one that was made almost literally on his own doorstep in Ruthwell. The parish church at Ruthwell lies surrounded by fields about a quarter of a mile outside the village. Although outwardly unremarkable, the church is unique in housing what is regarded as probably Scotland's finest Dark Age runic monument: the seventh- or eighth-century Ruthwell Cross. For well over a century now, the cross has held pride of place inside the church, where it can be seen in all its restored glory. Its panels

The Ruthwell Cross, standing in its purpose-built apse inside Ruthwell Church.

are decorated and carved with scenes from the life of Christ, and with lines from the Old English poem, 'The Dream of the Rood'. But since it was sculpted and engraved more than twelve centuries ago, the Ruthwell Cross has endured a very chequered history indeed.

The origins of the cross are cloaked in some mystery. For example, it is not known exactly who made it or precisely when it was fashioned, but it was certainly hewn from local stone. It was most probably used initially as a preaching cross: a place out of doors where people would gather for worship in the days before a church was built on the site. The consecrated ground surrounding it would have been used as a primitive form of graveyard and, later, when a stone-walled church was eventually built at Ruthwell, it was actually constructed around the cross and left partly unroofed to accommodate its height. In this way, the monument remained intact for many centuries.

However, in 1642, during the religious upheaval of Charles I's reign, the General Assembly of the Church of Scotland ordered that the cross should be destroyed, as it was deemed to be an 'idolatrous object'. Fortunately, the Revd Gavin Young, who was the minister at that time, arranged for it merely to be broken into sections and buried in the earthen floor of the church, rather than being dashed to smithereens. And there, hidden from view, the fragments of the cross remained for more than a century.

Eventually, during the 1780s, when some extensive renovation work was being carried out inside the church, including the laying of stone flags, the broken sections of the cross were brought to light, only to be instantly discarded in the churchyard, where they lay partly hidden for many years. It was left to the Revd Henry Duncan to recognise the historical and religious significance of the cross. For a number of years after arriving in Ruthwell, Duncan had been intrigued by the pieces of red and grey sandstone lying unheeded among the graves in the unkempt grass. He was particularly fascinated by the carvings and inscriptions that were still visible on the scattered pieces. 'Nothing could exceed the care bestowed by [Duncan] from year to year in deciphering the curious inscriptions,' the *Memoir* informs us, 'clearing from them the moss, and endeavouring to ascertain the meaning of the singular symbols and figures which crowd every inch of its surface.'

With the help of skilled craftsmen, and by exercising a great deal of patience, Duncan was eventually able to reassemble the column, although it became necessary to add a new crossbeam as the original one was never found. When the restoration work was completed in 1823, the Ruthwell Cross was erected in the garden of the manse where, for sixty years, it stood exposed to the not inconsiderable force of the elements on that unsheltered coastal strip.

In 1887, the cross was finally moved back inside the church. During his time as Ruthwell's minister (where he served from 1871 to 1889), the Revd James McFarlan was concerned that the frequent pounding by wind and rain would eventually cause irreparable damage to this important ancient monument. To prevent this from happening, it was even suggested at one stage that the cross should be housed at the Museum of Scotland, in Edinburgh. However, fortunately – because it is always more rewarding to view relics of this kind *in situ* – the move was averted when McFarlan was able to raise the necessary funds to have the column dismantled and re-erected inside the church. There it has remained ever since, standing in its purpose-built apse and providing a constant source of wonder for each new generation.

The remains of the Ruthwell Cross might easily have suffered a very different fate had it not been for the efforts of the Revd Henry Duncan, as the Secretary of the Society of Antiquaries of Scotland pointed out (in a letter quoted in the *Memoir*), after Duncan had submitted a paper on the subject to that distinguished body in 1832. 'Were more of our clergy than we can reckon upon at present as contributors to the society, to show but one half of the zeal which you have exhibited in this instance,' Duncan was told, 'the *Transactions of the Antiquaries of Scotland* would not suffer by a comparison with those of any similar body in Europe. Let us hope that your example will be followed.'

❧ ❧ ❧

Duncan's long years of painstaking work devoted to restoring and preserving for future generations the Ruthwell Cross, were sufficient to gain him a considerable reputation

The Savings Banks Museum, Ruthwell.

in his own right. Today, however, he is probably best-remembered around the globe as the so-called founding father of the savings banks movement, which began – to all intents and purposes – when Duncan opened his first ledger on 10 May 1810, in the long, low whitewashed cottage which stands at one end of Ruthwell's main street, and which now serves as the Savings Banks Museum. Inevitably, by the very nature of its singular claim, doubts have been expressed over the years that Duncan was the true originator of the savings banks scheme. This was a matter that Duncan's son sought to pre-empt in the *Memoir* of his father:

> It is not asserted that [Duncan] was the first to suggest it as possible for a labourer, or mechanic, or servant, under the ordinary circumstances of that class in this country, to make an important saving out of his or her weekly earnings – and as right in the richer classes to encourage this economy. Societies … consisting of wealthy and benevolent individuals, had in some instances been formed in different parts of England … to encourage the savings of the poor, by rewards, or an extraordinary rate of interest, furnished by the kind charity of the subscribers … The claim which we put forth for Mr Duncan to this title refers to the system in its national and public character … This was no scheme of charity … He rejoiced in the measure as calculated to inspire the labouring classes with a confidence in themselves, and hoped, by means of their industry and forethought, thus, ere long, to secure them to a great extent, even in old age, from requiring the begrudged and degrading bounty of a pauper's fund.

This building, in Church Crescent, Dumfries, with its statue of Duncan on the first floor, once housed the town's Savings Bank.

Like all the best ideas in our history, Duncan's scheme was a very simple one. It was put into action when the minister – finding himself in a struggling agricultural parish, where the farm labourer's daily wage was barely a shilling and unemployment an ever-present spectre – at first threw his energies into reviving the village's Friendly Society, which was in decline by the time he took up his ministry and which subsequently flourished under his supervision. Members paid in quarterly subscriptions to the society, in return for which they became entitled to various benefits, including sick pay when they were unable to go to work, and also funeral grants after a bereavement.

To Duncan, who had served part of a banking apprenticeship before entering the Church, it was an obvious extension of this scheme to encourage his parishioners to make what small savings they could out of their meagre weekly income. In a low-ceilinged room in the cottage that now receives visitors from all over the world, Duncan collected from the villagers those tiny amounts they could just afford to part with once their basic needs had been met; afterwards he deposited the money with the Linen Bank in Dumfries.

The chair that was specially made for Duncan by local estate workers in 1815.

At a time when the minimum deposit required by most − if not all − banks was £10, thus in effect making it impossible for ordinary working people such as the agricultural labourers of Ruthwell to ever open an account of their own, the advantages of Duncan's simple plan can be seen at once. At the end of each financial year, he redistributed the amounts saved together with the interest earned over the previous twelve months, only keeping sufficient money in reserve for a surplus fund to meet the cost of overheads. It was on the commercial principle of the Ruthwell scheme that the savings banks movement flourished and grew into the considerable force that it subsequently became.

By 1818, more than 130 similar small savings banks, each of them operating on the lines of Henry Duncan's Ruthwell model, had grown up in Scotland alone, with many more having opened in England and Wales. The idea spread rapidly throughout the land by word of mouth, in newspaper and magazine articles, and through the Church (for it should never be forgotten that, despite his other ventures and preoccupations, Duncan was first and foremost a dedicated parish minister). Eventually there were savings banks in Europe and the United States of America too. The first American bank to emulate Duncan's scheme was opened in Philadelphia in 1916. (In fact, the Philadelphia Savings Fund Society bore the Duncan tartan on the cover of its pass book for many years.)

The small Savings Banks Museum at Ruthwell, housed in premises that Duncan was able to persuade local landowner the Earl of Mansfield to build as a meeting place for the people of the village around 1800 (and called the Society Room), is owned and financed by Lloyds TSB. It was opened in 1974 to coincide with the bicentenary of Henry Duncan's birth and, among the items on display, are his desk and, of particular interest, the solid wooden chair in which he sat when receiving his parishioners' savings. It was specially made for him by local estate workers in 1815 at a cost of 18s 6d (£1.85). A large map of the world hangs on one wall, showing the countries to which the savings banks movement has spread across the globe.

Ruthwell's savings bank closed in 1876, and all the accounts were subsequently transferred to nearby Annan. By that time, the need for each village – or even hamlet – to maintain its own tiny branch was receding, as communities gradually became more mobile, especially after the proliferation of the railway system.

Since his death in 1846, Henry Duncan has undoubtedly been best-remembered by the world at large for his restoration work on the Ruthwell Cross and, in particular, for his founding of the savings banks movement. But most of his life was devoted to the parishioners and duties of the remote Solway parish that he served for almost half a century, and where he made such a favourable impression on those people around him.

Concluding the *Memoir*, published two years after his father's death, George Duncan wrote of him affectionately:

> He is already beyond the parish of Ruthwell, and has traversed the country which for forty-seven years was gladdened by [his] benevolence and zeal ... The soil is not particularly fertile, and the landscape possesses few engaging features; but in the eyes of those who knew him, its scenery can never be divested of a colouring, more lovely than the richest garniture of nature could have given it.

❧ FIVE ❧

THOMAS CARLYLE:
'AN ANNANDALE PEASANT'

In early February 1881, following his death during the first week of that dark and wintry month, the body of Thomas Carlyle was taken from his home of nearly fifty years in London and returned to his native Dumfriesshire village for burial in the local churchyard. As his friend and biographer J.A. Froude movingly described it, 'he was taken down in the night by the railway … snow had fallen, and road and field were wrapped in a white winding-sheet. The hearse, with the coffin, stood solitary in the station yard …'

Thomas Carlyle became one of the nineteenth century's most distinguished men of letters. Historian, philosopher, biographer and essayist, by the time of his death at 24 Cheyne Row he had become known affectionately as 'the Sage of Chelsea'. His major works included a three-volume *History of the French Revolution* (1837), *The Life and Letters of Oliver Cromwell* (1845), and the enormous six-volume biography *Frederick the Great* (1858-65), which reputedly took him fourteen years to complete and which, in his *Reminiscences*, he described himself 'wrestling with … as with the ugliest dragon which blotted out all the daylight and the rest of the world to me, till I should get it slain.'

However, these and Carlyle's many other considerable achievements were undreamt of when, in December 1795, he was born the son of a stonemason (who later turned farmer) in the small – and then newly-built – Arched House at Ecclefechan, five or so miles south-east of Lockerbie. Safely in the hands of the National Trust for Scotland, this pocket-handkerchief-sized cottage is now a museum and, as such, much visited by people from all over the world who are interested in Carlyle's life and work. The intrepid reader will be rewarded with some glimpses of Ecclefechan itself – or 'Entepfuhl' as he calls it – in Carlyle's semi-autobiographical, but perhaps to some modern eyes often impenetrable, *Sartor Resartus*, which first appeared as a volume in Britain in 1838 (although it had been issued in the United States two years earlier).

J.M. Sloan, writing in *The Carlyle Country* (1904), gives a description of Ecclefechan as it appeared around the time of Carlyle's birth:

The Arched House, Ecclefechan

[It] consisted mainly of two long rows of small cottages, roofed with thatch, situated on either side of the coach-road between London and Glasgow, sixteen miles north of Carlisle. There were no large houses then in the village; the most substantial building probably was the 'arch house' [*sic*] ... Trees were numerous in the village. The space occupied by the open burn kept the street wide, and made ample room for the elements of an unspeakable 'hurly burly' at the fairs.

Carlyle went to the local village school in Ecclefechan before, less happily, attending Annan Academy (the 'Hinterschlag Gymnasium' of *Sartor Resartus*) for three years from the age of eleven. Looking back on this period from the perspective of old age, he described it as '... very miserable, harsh, barren and worse ...' His teachers, he declared in *Sartor Resartus* (perhaps reflecting his thoughts about the Academy?) ...

... were hide-bound Pedants, without knowledge of man's nature or of boy's; or of aught save their lexicons and quarterly account-books ... Alas, the kind beech-rows of Entepfuhl were hidden in the distance: I was among strangers, harshly, at best indifferently, disposed towards me; the young heart felt, for the first time, quite orphaned and alone ... they were Boys ... and obeyed the impulse of rude Nature, which bids the deer-herd fall upon any stricken hart, the duck-flock put to death any broken-winged brother or sister, and on all hands the strong tyrannise over the weak.

Perhaps some measure of relief came in the dreary early winter of 1809, when fourteen-year-old Carlyle left home to walk a distance of over eighty miles north from Ecclefechan to Edinburgh, where he was due to take up his place at the university. Being so young, he did not travel alone; a slightly older local boy called Tom Smail made the arduous three-day trek with him. 'How strangely vivid, how remote and wonderful, tinged with the hues of far-off love and sadness, is that journey to me now,' recalled Carlyle in his *Reminiscences*:

> My mother and father walking with me in the dark, frosty November morning, through the village, to set us on our way … I hid my sorrow and my weariness, but had abundance of it chequering the mysterious hopes and forecastings of what Edinburgh and the student element would be.

Originally destined to enter the Church, Carlyle spent the next four years as a student in the Scottish capital, returning to the Arched House at Ecclefechan during the holidays and, later, to nearby Mainhill after his father had given up his old occupation and gone into farming. 'The road from Ecclefechan to Mainhill affords a most interesting climb,' wrote Sloan. 'At each fresh point of view in the ascent, it commands an outlook full of picturesque features – the comfortably wooded holm watered by the River Annan; the lower hills around Hoddom; Criffel in the west … the Cumberland mountains, with the Solway's belt of shining waters separating the two shores.' Froude noted crisply that 'the situation [of Mainhill] is high, utterly bleak and swept by all the winds …The view alone redeems the dreariness of the situation.'

Carlyle left university without taking his degree and he also abandoned any plans to enter the Church. Instead, he returned home and briefly taught mathematics at Annan Academy, before transferring to another teaching post in Kirkcaldy at a higher salary. He employed his time usefully during the school holidays by reading widely in German and English literature; a practice that would shape the course of his future life. He supplemented his teacher's salary with various kinds of literary hack work, and began contributing articles to the *Edinburgh Encyclopaedia*. He also translated from the French a book called *Elements of Geometry*, earning a useful fee of £50 in the process.

In 1818, Carlyle was back in Edinburgh intent on studying the law and possibly making it his future profession. He had managed to save up a small lump sum to live on, and he occasionally earned some extra cash from his freelance literary work. However, his circumstances were vastly improved in 1822 when he was engaged as a private tutor to two boys at the handsome annual salary of £200. 'This was a most important thing to me, in the economics and practical departments of my life,' declared Carlyle. All thoughts of the law were soon laid to one side, and he set about making a career from writing.

In the meantime, however, probably by far the most significant event in Carlyle's personal life had occurred in 1821, when he had been introduced to the woman who would eventually become his wife, Jane Baillie Welsh, the daughter of a general practitioner at Haddington in East Lothian. They were not married until five years later when, on 17 October 1826, the little wedding party assembled at Templand, near Thornhill, an early eighteenth-century farmhouse which was the home of Jane's grandfather, Walter Welsh, and the place where the marriage ceremony was performed. 'Carlyle wore the traditional white gloves,' observed Sloan, 'and never bridegroom more thoroughly merited such hymeneal adornments. So private a wedding was rare in Nithsdale. The young couple – Carlyle was 31, Jane Welsh 25 – left Templand by the coach the same day …'

Templand, near Thornhill, where the Carlyles were married in October 1826.

The couple remained very fond of Templand and Carlyle was particularly attracted by its beautiful surroundings:

> Keir, Penpont, Tynron lying spread, across the river, all as in a map, full of cheerful habitations, gentlemen's mansions, well-cultivated Farms and their cottages and appendages; spreading up in irregular slopes and gorges against the finest range of Hills …

The Carlyles were destined to make many return visits to Templand over the years, when they travelled back to Dumfriesshire for holidays from their home in London. They would sometimes stay at nearby Holmhill with their friends the Russells, whose home it was, and from where – as Joseph Laing Waugh recounted in *Thornhill and Its Worthies* (1913) – Mrs Carlyle would often be driven the short distance over to Templand:

> It held many dear old associations and sunny memories, and she scarcely ever left with a dry cheek. There was a little corner in the garden which seemed specially dear to her, and to which she always retired, standing away from everyone – silent and thoughtful.

Meanwhile, back at Holmhill, Carlyle always took delight in the Russells' garden, as Waugh explained:

> [He] had a favourite spot in the grounds to which he frequently retired. Here, under a tree, Dr. Russell instructed his 'man', Andrew Hunter, to make a seat, and … a chair-like rest was formed … He sat there for hours at a stretch smoking a long churchwarden pipe, unconscious of the excitement his great presence caused, and deaf to all entreaties to go inside and meet the many high-born visitors who called to pay their respects.

Following their wedding at Templand, the couple settled into their first home together at Comely Bank in Edinburgh, where Carlyle declared himself 'much happier than such a fool as I deserves to be.' In 1825, his *Life of Schiller* (the German dramatist and poet) had appeared in book form after being serialised in the *London Magazine*, and he had also been commissioned by an Edinburgh publisher to make a translation of Goethe's *Wilhelm Meister*. In the meantime, the newly-married Carlyles' daily pattern at Comely Bank crystallised into a routine that would eventually reach its full maturity during their long years together in Chelsea, with Jane presiding over the sundry concerns of the household while at the same time striving valiantly to shield her husband from the everyday distractions and irritations of domestic life that played so heavily on his nerves and destroyed his concentration, making it almost impossible for him to write. His particular bugbears at Cheyne Row, it would seem, were the sounds made by the neighbours' cockerels and pianos. In fact, neither of the Carlyles were immune to the distractions resulting from various kinds of noise, as Waugh noted:

> So nervous was Mrs Carlyle, and so highly strung her temperament, that the striking of the old eight-day clock [at Holmhill] annoyed her, as also did the early morning crowing of the farmyard roosters. The striking hammer was accordingly taken out of the works, and the cocks were banished during her stay.

In 1828, with the sound of another neighbour's bantam cock ringing in their ears, the Carlyles decided to leave Comely Bank, in fact to quit Edinburgh entirely. Money, or rather the lack of it, was probably their main reason for moving away from the city. Carlyle was no longer acting as a private tutor, and he would have been more secure financially with a profession behind him or a job of some kind to underpin his earnings from writing. The answer to their problems came in the form of Craigenputtock, a moorland farm about seven miles west of Dunscore, and a property that Jane had inherited from her father. Sloan writes that 'Carlyle had his eye upon Craigenputtock for several years, whereas Jane … was prejudiced against the place on account of its remoteness from civilized society.' However, not for the first – nor by any means the last – time in their lives together, Carlyle's will prevailed, and the couple duly took up residence there in May 1828. They stayed, with various interruptions, for six years, and it was here that Carlyle wrote *Sartor Resartus*, which was originally serialised in *Fraser's Magazine* (1833-34). Carlyle reflected in his *Reminiscences* that:

> We were not unhappy at Craigenputtock; perhaps these were our happiest days. Useful, continual labour, essentially successful; that makes even the moor green. I found I could do fully twice as much work in the given time there, as with my best effort was possible in London – such the interruptions etc. Once, in the winter time, I remember counting that for three months there had not any stranger, not even a beggar, called at Craigenputtock door. In summer we had sparsely visitors …

However, one of those summer visitors was the American poet and philosopher Ralph Waldo Emerson, who called at Craigenputtock during August 1833. 'I found the house amid desolate heathery hills where the lonely scholar nourished his mighty heart,' wrote Emerson in a letter. '… No public coach passed near it, so I took a private carriage from the inn …'

One senses, on the whole, that Carlyle's feelings for life at Craigenputtock as time rolled on veered between love and hate. As he put it, somewhat ambiguously, in his *Reminiscences* …

> … Of our history at Craigenputtock there might a great deal be written which might amuse the curious; for it was in fact a very singular scene and arena for such a pair as my Darling and me, with such a Life ahead; and bears some analogy to the settlement of Robinson Crusoe in his desert Isle, surrounded mostly by the wild populations, not wholly helpful or even harmless; and requiring, for its equipment into habitability and convenience, infinite contrivance, patient adjustment, and natural ingenuity in the head of Robinson himself … It looks to me now like a kind of humble russet-coated epic, that seven [*sic*] years' settlement at Craigenputtock; very poor in this world's goods, but not without an intrinsic dignity greater and more important than then appeared … I incline to think it the poor-best place that could have been selected for the ripening into fixity and composure, of anything useful which there may have been in me, against the years that were coming.

After leaving Craigenputtock in 1834 – a move no doubt dictated in part, at least, by the desire to be closer to the literary centre of things – Carlyle would never again be a full-time resident in his native county, although he still had almost half a century to live. He had toyed with the possibility of returning to live in Edinburgh, while lodging in the city for a few months during the winter of 1833 and gathering material for his proposed book about the French Revolution. In the end, however, he decided in favour of a move to London instead, where the Carlyles settled into what would become a long life together at Cheyne Row.

☙ ☙ ☙

The success of Carlyle's principal works, together with an impressive body of miscellaneous prose on social, historical and philosophical matters, meant that he acquired a reputation both at home and abroad as a great thinker and a towering literary figure. The novelist George Eliot wrote, in 1855, that 'there is hardly a superior or active mind of this generation that has not been modified by Carlyle's writings; there has hardly been an English book written for the last ten or twelve years that would not have been different if Carlyle had not lived.

Of Jane, who died in 1866, we have glimpsed little in this account of her husband. Nowadays we celebrate her as a literary figure in her own right, for the numerous and entertaining letters that poured out of her, but her friends and contemporaries knew her best as an accomplished hostess. Froude recalled that:

> [Carlyle's] wife had a genius for small evening entertainments, little tea parties such as in after days the survivors of us remember in Cheyne Row, over which she presided with

Dock Park in the autumn.

a grace all her own, and where wit and humour were to be heard flashing in no other house we ever found or hoped to find …

Despite living in London, Carlyle remained a loyal visitor to Dumfriesshire during the rest of his life. He would often call in at Dumfries itself, where he not only had family connections but had also become friends with Thomas Aird: poet, essayist and editor of the *Dumfries Courier*. The two men, reported Sloan, 'often walked and talked together in the Dock Park by the river's bank.' Even during the fifteen years that were left to him after Jane's death, Carlyle remained a familiar sight in Dumfries during his summer visits from London. 'Towards the end,' continued Sloan, 'when the burden of natural senility was becoming all too heavy for him, difficulty was experienced in obtaining such a house for him anywhere hereabouts as might be sufficiently remote from the noise of railways, and beyond earshot of the cock's crow at dawn.'

Following Thomas Carlyle's death at Cheyne Row, he was conveyed home for a final time in accordance with his own last wishes. Given his eminence, Westminster Abbey would have been his natural resting-place, but he wanted to be buried beside his mother and so his body was returned to the village of his birth. A report in the *Dumfries and Galloway Standard* on 12 February 1881 stated that:

> Dumfriesshire received to her parent bosom one of her most illustrious sons, [when] the mortal remains of Thomas Carlyle were … laid with kindred dust, and amid the hallowed scenes of his childhood years, in the quiet old churchyard of Ecclefechan … The journey

Carlyle is buried just a short step away from his childhood home.

The statue of Carlyle at Ecclefechan.

[north] made in the shadowy moonlight, the approach of the sad burden being heralded by the wild shriek of the engine and the glare of the furnace, was a not unfitting scene in the last Act of the life of one who is such a striking figure in the literary history of his age.

Sloan describes how, at the last:

> ... no religious service is read, no prayers are offered. In silent fortitude the coffin is lowered into the grave by the nearest relatives, according to Scottish custom. Thomas Carlyle is buried as he was born, as he lived – an Annandale peasant elevated through the dynamic forces of culture, transfigured by self-devotion to Truth and to the Cause of Man.

Carlyle's connection with Ecclefechan is immediately made apparent to anyone entering the village today, even though his name might have been previously unfamiliar to them. In 1927, a large statue depicting the great man seated – a replica of that executed during the 1870s by the sculptor Sir Joseph Boehm and erected between Cheyne Row and the Albert Embankment in Chelsea – was placed at the top of the hill leading down into Ecclefechan from the north. Despite his great fame and international reputation Carlyle never forgot his roots, so that even in death his impressive figure presides over the small Annandale village where he was born.

❧ SIX ❧

MOFFAT:
THE 'CHELTENHAM OF SCOTLAND'

Think of popular spa resorts, and places such as Bath, Cheltenham and Harrogate immediately spring to mind. Moffat would almost certainly not feature very prominently – if, indeed, at all – on most people's list of once-fashionable and thriving watering-places. However, there was a time, not so far distant, when this small Annandale town enjoyed for many years an enviable reputation as the 'Cheltenham of Scotland'. Dominated by Hart Fell, which rises to almost 2,700ft above sea level, Moffat lies on the upper reaches of the River Annan, tucked into a fold of the Southern Uplands towards the north-east corner of Dumfries and Galloway. A nineteenth-century *Gazeteer of Scotland* described it as 'one of the prettiest small towns in Scotland.'

Set in an area of great natural charm, Moffat has something of a dilemma: is it a holiday destination in its own right, or more often simply a convenient overnight port of call for travellers making their way from the south to the undeniably more spectacular Highlands? (This is not to imply that the country around Moffat is short of natural spectacles. There is the Devil's Beef Tub, for example, and the Grey Mare's Tail ten miles or so north-east of the town. This famous waterfall – described by Sir Walter Scott in his long poem 'Marmion' as 'white as the snowy charger's tail' – issues out of lonely Loch Skeen, and drops 300ft before emptying into Moffat Water.) Local tourist information has sometimes been a touch ambiguous about Moffat's role over the years, such as when describing the town as 'the Gateway to Scotland' – a phrase that does little to clarify its position. Certainly there is no shortage of good reasons for the visitor to linger, as *Fairfoul's Guide to Moffat*, first published in 1876 and reissued a few years later, was not slow to point out. Among the manifold advantages of the town were:

> … the medicinal virtues of its spas … its pure air and invigorating climate, derived from the healthful breezes in constant circulation among the neighbouring hills … the charming variety of scenery – hill and valley, wood and water – recurring in rapid succession …

Lonely Loch Skeen in winter.

the number and variety of walks, rides and drives … the numerous eminences in the immediate neighbourhood … [and] the picturesque site of the town.

On an interesting literary note, Fairfoul points out that Moffat '… is a connecting link between the land of Burns on the west, and the land of Scott and Hogg on the east, and each member of this illustrious trio has left his mark on places which soon become familiar to the visitor.' In a celebrated incident, Scott and James Hogg, the Ettrick Shepherd, almost came to grief while riding over the notoriously hazardous peaty terrain on the margins of Loch Skeen, among the dark scenery that Scott drew on not only in 'Marmion' but also in his novel *Old Mortality*. Scott and Hogg had probably set off from one of their favourite haunts, Tibbie Shiel's Inn, a few miles further to the east along the Selkirk road at St Mary's Loch. They would almost certainly have begun their ascent on the still relatively little-used path from Birkhill, picking their way gingerly over by Watch Knowe – a useful look-out post for Covenanters during the seventeenth century – where the ground is riddled with huge sink-holes to this day. It is recorded in J.G. Lockhart's biography of Scott (who was the biographer's father-in-law), that Scott and his horse fell into a bog and only got out again with some difficulty. Scott managed it somehow and, recalled Hogg, 'we went to Moffat that night … and such a night of glee I never witnessed.'

☙ ☙ ☙

Moffat's broad High Street, pictured here early on a Sunday morning.

Moffat's hub is the High Street, '... judiciously laid out, spacious, and well calculated to form an agreeable promenade for both inhabitants and strangers', according to the nineteenth-century *Gazeteer*. It is said to be one of the broadest high streets in Scotland, and it is certainly wide enough to accommodate a substantial central aisle, which nowadays serves as a busy – and to the constant delight of surprised tourists, free – car park. Here, the Colvin Fountain presides over the scene. The pedestal of red Corncockle sandstone, capped by the bronze statue of a ram, was presented to the town by William Colvin of nearby Beattock, and stands on the site of Moffat's former renowned bowling green. Dominating the High Street, the ram is a constant reminder of the town's connection with sheep and wool – something which is also recalled annually in early July, with the installation of the Shepherd and Lass on the eve of Gala Day, at a ceremony held in front of the Town Hall.

Not even the most transient of visitors could fail to notice that Moffat abounds with hotels, each with a character and atmosphere of its own. There is the 'Black Bull', for example, which originally dates from the seventeenth century and can claim to be one of Moffat's oldest buildings. For several years during the 'Killing Times' it served as the headquarters of 'Bloody' Claverhouse, when he hunted down the scores of Covenanters who took refuge in the surrounding hills while defending their religious beliefs. Robert Burns once scratched a verse on one of the Black Bull's window-panes; it was an epigram on Miss Deborah Davies, with whom the poet had become acquainted when living at Ellisland:

Ask why God made the gem so small?
And why so huge the granite? –
Because God meant mankind should set
That higher value on it.

The original inscribed glass was later removed, but a replica window bearing a facsimile of the lines was unveiled at the Black Bull in 1996, the bicentenary year of Burns's death.

The High Street can boast the much-photographed nineteenth-century Star Hotel, which has been officially recognised by the *Guinness Book of Records* as the narrowest detached hotel in the world and, on the other side of the road, the elegance of Moffat House Hotel, designed by John Adam and built in the 1760s as a private residence for the second Earl of Hopetoun. These, together with other hotels such as the Annandale Arms and the Balmoral, for example, both of them dating from the eighteenth century, evoke those palmy days of Moffat's popularity as a watering-place.

Moffat's gradual transformation from an ordinary Annandale village going about its everyday business, to its eventual eminence as the 'Cheltenham of Scotland', began quietly enough in 1633, when Rachel Whiteford – 'daughter of Dr Walter Whiteford', *Fairfoul's Guide* informs us, 'a man of distinguished abilities, parson of Moffat at that time, and next year promoted to the diocese of Brechin ...' – discovered a sulphurous well when she was out walking beyond what are now the northern outskirts of the town. It may be an exaggeration to say that, following Rachel Whiteford's discovery, the fortunes of Moffat were changed overnight but, by the middle of the eighteenth

The Star Hotel.

century, the town was firmly established as Scotland's answer to Cheltenham. It is interesting to note that Cheltenham's own origins as a famous watering-place were equally low-key. In 1716, the presence of a flock of pigeons feeding on grains of salt in a meadow now occupied by Cheltenham Ladies' College, brought to light a saline spring, the water from which was promptly sold for medicinal purposes by the meadow's owner. Later, in 1738, a small pump room was built over the spring, although it would be more than fifty years before Cheltenham's reputation as a spa resort was finally confirmed.

Early morning became the most popular time for 'taking the waters' at Moffat and, during the summer season, a long procession of people – often 200 or 300 strong (hence, perhaps, a good reason for Moffat's thriving hotel trade) – could be found every day, making its way along the winding lane leading from the town up to the well, where the visitors drank their 'statutory quantum' of three large tumblers of water. 'A man of moderate energies … may take his three tumblers without being inconvenienced,' averred Fairfoul, 'but on the contrary braced and appetised, though he should not be in any undue haste to run to his breakfast.' The whole operation was often performed to the accompaniment of local musicians. Fairfoul continued:

> [A] fair moiety of the Moffat visitors are supposed to have been there and got back again to their lodgings before breakfast … A few of the more enthusiastic well-goers are always forward between six and seven o'clock, but it is not till half-past seven that there is anything of a throng. About that time, the hotel omnibuses, usually well freighted, have delivered their companies; there are commonly also several private conveyances drawing up about the same time. The pedestrians … have visibly increased; and the scene in a short time gets exceedingly animated. The verandah is filled to overflowing, and the rustic seats and the grassy bank in front are clad with ladies and gentlemen.
>
> The water is served in tumblers at a sort of counter drawn across the verandah in front of the well house. From the general eagerness, and obvious pressure to be forward and served, the drinking of the water evidently is, as it ought to be, a very important matter with the bulk of the company. There are many, however, who are chiefly there for the walk's sake, and the agreeable excitement of so lively a scene … A habit of a large number of drinkers is to sit, or walk slowly about, tumbler in hand, sipping the contents very leisurely. The water always loses by this delay, as the free sulphuretted hydrogen gas, which is one of its characteristic and most valuable constituents, commences to disengage itself the moment it comes in contact with the atmosphere. The water itself, on a few hours' open exposure, becomes flat and insipid and void of flavour.

In 1748, a chalybeate spring was discovered by John Williamson under the bulk of Hart Fell. In contrast to the sulphurous water of Moffat Well, the liquid obtained from Hart Fell Spa retained its original quality over a long period of time and was, in fact, dispatched as far afield as the West Indies. No doubt it also tasted better than the liquid drawn from Moffat Well whose flavour, as Fairfoul recorded, 'has been likened to that of bilge water, of rotten eggs and of a gun newly fired', although he goes on to say (rather charitably, some people might think) that 'the mildest of these comparisons no doubt exaggerates … in the long run there is no water goes more pleasantly down.'

The supposed healing properties of Moffat's spa water were trumpeted far and wide, and people flocked to the town not only to drink this seemingly health-promoting liquid but to bathe in it as well. At first, this was only made possible by the enterprise of a local woman who hired out deep wooden tubs for the purpose. A carter brought the sulphurous water down from the well into the town, where the tubs were filled so that the visitors could bathe in the privacy of their own rooms. Later, in 1827, an imposing Baths House was built in the classical style of the period, complete with Doric columns and portico, and to which the water was conveyed by pipe from the well. The Baths House contained reading rooms, bathing apartments and an assembly room where concerts were held.

The vast Moffat Hydropathic Hotel, set in a commanding position overlooking Annan Water was, with its 300 or so rooms, ample confirmation – were it required – of Moffat's status as the 'Cheltenham of Scotland'. Opened on 5 April 1878, when Moffat's reputation as a spa resort was still at its height, the Hydro was regarded as one of the largest and best equipped institutions of its kind anywhere in Britain. Administered by the Moffat Hydropathic Company and designed in the French Renaissance style, it was built of sandstone extracted from the quarries at Locharbriggs, Corncockle and Newton. The overall cost was estimated at around £87,000, including furnishings and the price of the land on which the building stood. 'The house is of great extent,' enthused Fairfoul, 'and for this reason, as well as the style of architecture, the effect is grand and imposing … The public rooms are airy and spacious, and the accommodation for residents of the most comfortable and attractive description.'

Moffat received a further boost to its fortunes only five years later when, in the spring of 1883, the town was at last linked to the main west coast railway line at Beattock. The journey took only six minutes and could be enjoyed, in those far-off days, for a mere 2*d* (with a return fare of 3*d*). 'By completion of the little branch line from Beattock,' gushed the local newspaper, 'the fashionable watering-place of Moffat has been brought fairly into contact with the railway system, and the line cannot fail to be of great advantage to the hosts of visitors who resort to Moffat in summer.' All the main line trains which stopped at Beattock – originally operated by the Caledonian Railway and from the early 1920s by London, Midland and Scottish – had connections to and from Moffat.

Moffat's station and the line to Beattock were eventually closed to passengers in 1954, and the once familiar and still fondly recalled shout of 'Beattock for Moffat', which had guided scurrying passengers for decades from the main line platform to their branch line connection, was silenced for ever, although goods traffic continued on the route into the 1960s.

Sadly, within just a few decades of the Hydropathic opening, and despite the town's new-found accessibility by rail, the number of people arriving at Moffat to 'take the waters' – hitherto thousands each season – began to decline, and the Hydro changed hands several times. During the First World War it was used as a military convalescent

Hart Fell. Hart Fell Spa lies at the foot of the cleft in the hills seen here on the right.

home for officers. Then, in the early hours of Monday 2 June 1921, the Hydro burned to the ground, in what was thought to be one of the worst fires ever seen in Dumfriesshire up to that time. On the night in question, around 140 people – guests and staff – were in residence but, miraculously, everyone escaped from the building more or less unharmed. The local newspaper reported that:

> Large numbers of the townspeople of Moffat were attracted to the scene of the outbreak very early in the morning and they very kindly gave assistance in trying to alleviate the hardships of the visitors, who had to make such a hurried escape from the burning building. In a good many cases clothing had to be procured for those who had rushed from their rooms clad only in their night attire, and numbers of the visitors were temporarily accommodated in adjacent residences and boarding-houses until the morning, when they returned to their homes by rail or motorcar.

The cause of the fire remained a mystery, although there was some speculation that the roof timbers may have been smouldering for some time, having perhaps been ignited by a stray spark from a chimney fire.

Although labelled the 'Cheltenham of Scotland', Moffat seems to have weathered its years of great popularity without attracting the worst kind of visitors which, according to that arch agitator, William Cobbett, were commonly to be found frequenting that fine Gloucestershire spa resort; '… a place,' he claimed, after paying it a visit in September 1826, 'to which East India plunderers, West India floggers, English tax-gorgers, together with gluttons, drunkards and debauchees of all descriptions, female as well as male, resort, at the suggestion of silently laughing quacks, in the hope of getting rid of the bodily consequences of their manifold sins and iniquities. To places like this,' he went on, 'come all that is knavish and all that is foolish and all that is base; gangsters, pick-pockets and harlots; young wife-hunters in search of rich and ugly old women, and young husband-hunters in search of rich and wrinkled or half-rotten men.'

Above: *Moffat's former Baths House.* Left: *All that remains of Moffat Well today.*

Whether or not the observations to be found in this outpouring of bile were drawn from any kind of methodical research or were merely the result of an unshakeable personal prejudice is left to Cobbett's readers to decide but, understandably, the good people of Cheltenham and the patrons of its efficacious waters were not amused by this unseemly outburst, and took their revenge on Cobbett by carrying a burning effigy of him through the streets of the town.

❧ ❧ ❧

Walking through Moffat's High Street today, it is odd to think that the town once ranked so highly as a spa resort (although the keen-eyed observer will notice street names such as Well Road and Hydro Avenue). The Baths House, once the scene of concerts and assemblies has, in more recent years, housed – somewhat prosaically – the Town Hall and public library. Of the well itself only the shaft remains, although the small stone building which houses it was restored in 1986. Nevertheless, the setting is still attractive: perched on the edge of a small ravine, and reached by the same quiet lane winding up, through fields of sheep and cattle, from the town.

❧ SEVEN ❧

WANLOCKHEAD: SCOTLAND'S HIGHEST VILLAGE

It may come as a surprise to some people to learn that the highest inhabited village in Scotland can be found not among the rugged mountain landscapes of the Cairngorms or West Highlands, but in the rolling Southern Uplands.

Wanlockhead, eight miles or so east of Sanquhar, stands at around 1,500ft above sea level among the Lowther Hills, at the head of the winding Mennock Pass. Writing in his book, *The History of Sanquhar* (1891), James Brown has provided us with a vivid description of this spectacular route:

> In truth, so high and wild is this Mennock road that in winter it is no uncommon occurrence for vehicular traffic to be entirely suspended, leaving the telegraph as the only mode of communication with the outer world available to the inhabitants of Wanlockhead ... In the summer season, however, its alpine scenery makes it one of the finest drives in the district, presenting, as it does, features of wild grandeur and peculiar configuration of hill not surpassed even in the West Highlands ... Wanlockhead comes into sight quite suddenly and unexpectedly. For miles no human dwelling has been visible, nor sound heard save the murmur of the stream, the bleating of the sheep, and the whirr of the grouse or blackcock as, on strong wing, he sweeps across the glen and drops out of sight among the deep heather which covers the mountain sides.

Even measured by present-day standards, Wanlockhead could still be regarded as something of an isolated community, especially in the depths of winter, when the climate can often prove to be harsh and uncompromising in this rugged environment. However, Wanlockhead can lay claim to far more than just its unique geographical distinction. Unrelenting though that environment may sometimes be, the village grew into existence as a result of the valuable natural underground deposits on which it stands, and which can also be found in the surrounding hills; because here – and at neighbouring Leadhills, less than two miles away – lead has been mined intermittently to a greater or lesser extent, possibly even since the days of the Roman occupation.

The village sign is much photographed by tourists.

However, it was not until the eighteenth century that an efficiently organised and substantial commercial industry could be said to have fully developed.

In his lengthy account of lead-mining in the area, published in 1838 (and included in Brown's *History of Sanquhar*), Dr Watson of Wanlockhead explains – perhaps in somewhat too complex detail for the layman to readily understand – the succession of companies and individuals into whose hands fell the leases for working the mines towards the end of the seventeenth and during the first half of the eighteenth century. The following brief extracts will give the reader a flavour of his work, but for any serious student of mining in the area his full account would prove invaluable:

> Sir James Stampfield was the first person who, about the year 1680, opened … up [the mines] … Mathew Wilson [succeeded] him in the year 1691, and had a lease for nineteen years. The Governor and Company for smelting down lead ore with coal succeeded Mathew Wilson in the year 1710. They had a lease for thirty-one years … In the year 1721, several gentlemen of London, Newcastle and Edinburgh, having united under the name of the Friendly Mining Society, entered into partnership with the Smelting Company, for carrying on the mines of Wanlockhead upon a further lease of thirty-one years … The Friendly Society carried on their workings … till the year 1734; at which time, having ascertained that they had been great losers, although they had raised a valuable quantity of lead ore, they resigned their lease, and were succeeded by William and Alexander Telfer … [Following William's death] … Alexander Telfer was succeeded by Messrs Ronald Crawford and Company (now the Wanlockhead Mining Company) in the year 1755; they being gentlemen not only of capital, but of great enterprise, have had several of the principal veins prosecuted not only vigorously, but most judiciously, and to a great extent …

In a slightly later account (once again included in Brown's *History of Sanquhar*), Mr Edmond, a Wanlockhead schoolmaster, explained how …

... towards the close of the lease of the Wanlockhead Mining Company, the mines were in a great measure unproductive. Few workmen were employed, the machinery was mostly primitive and worn out, and the prospect of successful mining most hopeless. In 1842, the Duke of Buccleuch [owner of the land in question] took the mines under his own care. Skilful management, with new and improved machinery, led to the opening out of veins that yielded largely and steadily for years, bringing profit to the proprietor and prosperity generally to the village.

At the height of their output, the combined mines of Wanlockhead and Leadhills were said to account for about 80 per cent of all Scottish lead.

However, the deposits that were to be found locally were not exclusively confined to lead. Wanlockhead has attracted more than its fair share of prospectors over the centuries, owing to the fact that gold was discovered in the area during the Middle Ages. This remote corner of Dumfries and Galloway could hardly be said to have rivalled the Klondike, but the results of gold-panning over the course of 400 or so years (alongside a profitable lead-mining industry) have earned the area the enviable – if somewhat hyperbolical – title of 'God's Treasure-House in Scotland'. Writing in his book of that name, published in 1876, the Revd J. Moir Porteous recorded how a certain George Bowes ...

... [a] gold-seeker of eminence, who held a commission from Queen Elizabeth ... was empowered to dig and delve as he would; and that at Winlocke Head [*sic*] he discovered a small vaine [*sic*] of gold, which had much small gold upon it. He swore his men to secrecy, and after working the vein for some time he caused the shaft to be closed up, and took oath of his men to keep it concealed. The locality of this vein looked for and alluded to by several parties as never refound, is not unknown to the miners at Wanlockhead. Pieces of gold of 30oz weight were found in this neighbourhood in the reign of James V, mixed with the spar, some with keel, and some with brimstone.

Porteous goes on further to explain how the hapless Bowes ...

... returned to England [after finding more veins of gold in the area] with a purse of gold valued at seven-score pounds. The Queen of England was so encouraged by his success that he was commanded to return in spring to resume the search. But the spring returned not for George Bowes. Visiting mines in Cumberland, he turned aside to look, fell down a shaft, and was killed.

The Revd Thomas Hastings, in his *History of Wanlockhead* (written in 1862), tells how '... Sir Bevis Bulmer, Treasurer to Queen Elizabeth, who had obtained the consent of James the Sixth, was [at Wanlockhead] with a hundred men for several summers collecting gold by her orders, and they succeeded in finding some hundred thousand pounds' worth of gold.' Four centuries later, in 1992, Wanlockhead was the venue for the World Gold Panning Championships. Also, the British and Scottish Gold Panning Championships are regularly held here. (Anyone who is interested in learning the art

A present-day reminder of Wanlockhead's industrial 'golden age'.

of gold-panning would certainly benefit from taking part in one of the various courses on the subject offered by the village's Museum of Lead Mining, but it is essential to contact the museum beforehand regarding opening times and availability.)

Wanlockhead's industrial 'golden age' could fairly be said to have spanned the eighteenth and nineteenth centuries, and it would be easy to characterise a remote mining village of those days, tucked deep in the Lowther Hills, as a drab and uninviting – perhaps even hostile – place, but the evidence points to the contrary. 'The miners' houses are built in the most charmingly irregular order,' enthused Brown, writing in 1891. 'They lie for the most part round the base of the Dod Hill, from which the inhabitants are frequently nick-named 'the Dodders'. Originally all thatched with heather, a large number are now of modern construction and are roofed with slate ... They are very cosy and comfortable, and are inhabited by a remarkably strapping, fine-looking body of miners.' There was also a powerful sense of community spirit in the village (an almost invariable trait among mining communities everywhere), with a highly successful Co-operative Society being established in 1871 and, eight years later, the formation of a society 'for the relief of the aged and infirm ... Previous to that time,' as Brown explained:

> There was a kindly custom among the miners that, if one of a partnership died, his widow was allowed to enjoy the proceeds of what would have been her husband's share, after certain necessary deductions; if he left a son, the lad succeeded to his father's partnership. In this way, without parochial aid, the poor of the village were saved from feeling the pinch of poverty and hardship.

The physical health of the younger miners – Porteous described them as 'tall, strapping young men, strong and hardy' – was promoted by the aid of various open-air sporting

A row of traditional miners' cottages.

activities, probably the most popular of which was curling. 'Situated so high above sea-level, the Wanlockhead miners enjoy the game of curling much more frequently than their confreres anywhere else,' declared Brown, 'and better curlers can nowhere be found.'

Wanlockhead has enjoyed a variety of literary connections over the years. The eighteenth-century novelist, Tobias Smollett, for example, who was related by marriage to one of the partners in a local mining company, is reliably thought to have written at least a part of his last – and, some critics believe, finest – novel, *The Expedition of Humphry Clinker* (1771), while staying in the village during 1770, the year before his death. Written in the epistolary style that was in vogue at the time, the novel recounts – through a series of letters sent to friends and acquaintances of the characters involved – the wanderings of Matthew Bramble. Attended by a party which includes his niece and nephew, an elderly unmarried sister and their maidservant, he leaves home to scour the country in search of good health. Bramble's quest eventually takes him north to Edinburgh. As the party subsequently travelled south, making for home, they stopped at Drumlanrig Castle, (not many miles from Wanlockhead), as Smollet – in the guise of Bramble – related:

His Grace [the Duke of Queensberry] keeps open house, and lives with great splendour. He did us the honour to receive us with great courtesy, and detain'd us all night … The duchess was equally gracious, and took our ladies under her immediate protection … From Drumlanrig we pursued the course of the Nid [Nith] to Dumfries, which … is, after Glasgow, the handsomest town I have seen in Scotland.

The Mennock Pass.

Just over thirty years later, the poet William Wordsworth passed through Wanlockhead while enjoying a Scottish touring holiday with his sister, Dorothy, and their friend and fellow-poet, Samuel Taylor Coleridge. Travelling in an Irish jaunting-car, the trio was bound for Glasgow and other points further north, having just made a special pilgrimage to Burns's house and grave in Dumfries. Dorothy recorded her impressions of the trip in her journal, *Recollections of a Tour, Made in Scotland 1803.* She recalled how, when they left Thornhill to embark on their ascent of the Mennock Pass …

> … the road for a little way was very steep, bare hills with sheep … The simplicity of the prospect impressed us very much; we now felt indeed that we were in Scotland … There was no room in the vale but for the river and the road; we had sometimes the stream to the right, sometimes to the left …

Eventually reaching Wanlockhead, she described the village as '… a wild and singular spot'. The holiday party then encountered a small group of local children, as Dorothy duly noted:

> Just as we began to climb the hill we saw three boys who came down the cleft of a brow on our left … Our little lads before they had gone far were joined by some half-dozen of their companions, all without shoes and stockings … they went to school and learned Latin (Virgil) and some of them Greek (Homer), but when Coleridge began to inquire further, off they ran poor things! I suppose afraid of being examined.

Of course, Burns himself was not an infrequent visitor to Wanlockhead at one stage in his life, often being drawn to the village in his capacity as an exciseman.

One well-documented visit describes how he arrived there on a particularly cold day during the winter of 1789-90 and was unable at first to get his horse's shoes adapted for the icy conditions prevailing at that altitude, although the local blacksmith subsequently agreed to do the work. Burns was moved to compose some lines on the subject. 'Pegasus at Wanlockhead' (the poet's horse was called Pegasus) concludes:

> Obliging Vulcan fell to work,
> Threw by his coat and bonnet,
> And did Sol's business in a crack;
> Sol paid him with a sonnet.
>
> Ye Vulcan's sons of Wanlockhead,
> Pity my sad disaster;
> My Pegasus is poorly shod,
> I'll pay you like my master.

Together with Leadhills, Wanlockhead has also produced a respectable crop of home-grown literary talent. Probably the two most famous names to emerge from the locality are the poets Robert Reid and Allan Ramsay. Reid, who wrote under the pen-name 'Rab Wanlock', was born in Wanlock House in 1850. He died in Montreal in 1922, having emigrated to Canada during the late-1870s, and a commemorative plaque in his memory can be seen on the wall of Wanlockhead's Miners' Library. The concluding verse of his long poem, 'Wanlock', leaves the reader in no doubt of Reid's deep and abiding affection for his native place:

> Sangs tell aboot Yarrow and Doon's bonny braes,
> The Luggie rows saft in that measure o' Gray's;
> Frae Tweed tae the Beauly there's hardly a glen
> But it brags it has minstrels and rhymes o' its ain:
> Yet here's a wee toon never named in their glee,
> That's mair than them a' put thegither tae me.

Allan Ramsay was born at Leadhills almost 200 years earlier, in 1686. His most successful work, 'The Gentle Shepherd', much admired by James Boswell among others, appeared in 1725. As a young man he had begun work in Edinburgh as an apprentice wig-maker, eventually setting up his own business probably in the Grassmarket. However, by the early 1720s, he had already become known as a poet, and he turned from wig-making to bookselling as his occupation. 'His squat podgy figure waddling down the High Street on his way to the shop in the Luckenbooths, his head covered with the quaint three-cornered hat of the period,' wrote Oliphant Smeaton, in his biography of the poet published in 1896, 'was one of the familiar sights of Edinburgh, to be pointed out to strangers with a pride and affection that never diminished.'

✿ ✿ ✿

The Miners' Library.

Although Wanlockhead's mines have long since closed for commercial purposes – operations ceased in 1934, but one mine did open and close again during the 1950s – the village is a prospering and forward-looking community today, having imaginatively and successfully tailored much of its industrial heritage to the tourist market. Happily, this is a far cry from the situation that prevailed half a century ago, when the author of the *Third Statistical Account of Scotland (The County of Dumfries)* wrote of Wanlockhead in 1953 that:

> [Its] fortunes ... depend on the success or failure of the lead-making industry. [At present] there seems to be no prospect of an alternative industry being brought into the village. Should the present trend of events continue, it seems more than likely that, as a virile thriving community, Wanlockhead will cease to exist.

Visitors to the village – some of them walkers on the Southern Upland Way long-distance footpath which runs through the heart of Wanlockhead – are able to experience something of the local history for themselves at the Museum of Lead Mining and Visitor Centre, where machinery, tools and various relics covering over 250 years of lead-mining in the surrounding area can be seen. They may also, if so inclined, enjoy a guided tour of the Lochnell Visitor Mine, which was last worked during the 1860s. (These attractions are not open to the public throughout the year, so it is essential to check opening times to avoid disappointment.) In one sense, Wanlockhead itself could be seen as an open-air mining museum, with its traditional-style cottages dotted around the village; the Miners' Library, founded in 1756 and – as such – Europe's second oldest subscription library, which was much restored in the late-1990s and

Above: *The entrance to Lochnell Mine.* Below: *Wanlockhead's well-preserved Beam Engine is an impressive sight.*

contains around 3,000 books (many of them extremely rare); and the unique Beam Engine, which was used for mine drainage during the nineteenth century and is now an industrial monument. These, together with other interesting features linked to Wanlockhead's mining past, can be savoured by anyone who follows the 'Visitor Trail' in the village and immediate area.

❧ EIGHT ❧

KIRKCUDBRIGHT: THE ARTISTS' TOWN

'If one lives in Galloway,' observed Dorothy L. Sayers at the beginning of her detective novel *Five Red Herrings* (1931), 'one either fishes or paints.' Although it was an obvious over-simplification of the way of life in this quiet and thinly populated corner of south-west Scotland, nevertheless it is not difficult to understand what she was driving at. The Galloway landscape is a joy to behold; the light is generally deemed favourable for those people bent on artistic pursuits and, for the fisherman – amateur or professional – the Solway Coast is close at hand. When the poet John Keats passed through the area in the summer of 1818, during a prodigiously long walking tour with his friend Charles Armitage Brown, he declared that '… the country is very rich, very fine, and with a little of Devon'. Sayers wrote that:

> The artistic centre of Galloway is Kirkcudbright where the painters form a scattered constellation, whose nucleus is the High Street, and whose outer stars twinkle in remote hillside cottages, radiating brightness as far as Gatehouse-of-Fleet. There are large and stately studios, panelled and high, in strong stone houses … There are workaday studios … where a good north light and a litter of brushes and canvas form the whole of the artistic stock-in-trade. There are little homely studios … tucked away down narrow closes and adorned with gardens, where old-fashioned flowers riot in the rich and friendly soil. There are studios that are simply and solely barns, made beautiful by ample proportions and high-pitched rafters … There are artists who have large families and keep domestics in cap and apron; artists who engage rooms, and are taken care of by landladies; artists who live in couples or alone, with a woman who comes in to clean; artists who live hermit-like and do their own charing. There are painters in oils, painters in water-colours, painters in pastel, etchers and illustrators, workers in metal; artists of every variety, having this one thing in common – that they take their work seriously and have no time for amateurs.

It is apparent from this description of the place that Sayers was very well acquainted with, and attracted to, Kirkcudbright – a town where the creator of the aristocratic

The harbour at Kirkcudbright is flourishing today.

amateur sleuth Lord Peter Wimsey (a character memorably portrayed on television during the 1970s by Ian Carmichael), and her journalist husband 'Mac' Fleming, had spent their holidays for several years during the period between the First and Second World Wars. By this time, Kirkcudbright and the surrounding area had long become recognised for the large and somewhat amorphous group of artists that had been drawn there since before the close of the nineteenth century.

Two hundred or so years before Sayers made her distinctive mark on the town – Christopher Somerville, writing in his book *Twelve Literary Walks* (1985), explained that she was noted locally for her 'loud voice, wide-brimmed hat and long cigarette-holder' – Daniel Defoe, the author of *Robinson Crusoe* (1719), visited Kirkcudbright during the course of his monumental *Tour through the Whole Island of Great Britain*, noting on that occasion that the town had:

> A pleasant situation, and yet nothing pleasant to be seen. Here is a harbour without ships, a port without trade, a fishery without nets, a people without business; and, that which is worse than all, they do not seem to desire business … They have all the materials for trade, but no genius to it; all the opportunities for trade, but no inclination to it. In a word, they have no notion of being rich and populous, and thriving by commerce … It is true the reason is in part evident, namely poverty; no money to build vessels, hire seamen, buy nets and materials for fishing, to cure the fish when it is catched, or to carry it to market when it is cured; this discourages the mind, checks industry, and prevents all manner of application.

Although Defoe's account of his travels covering the length and breadth of the land – and comprising an early and important national survey, written with the eye and ear of a keen journalist – was published in three volumes between 1724 and 1726 (and only a few years before Defoe's death in 1731), the visit to Kirkcudbright would almost certainly have taken place some years earlier. Whatever the exact date may have been, Defoe's on-the-spot assessment was a decidedly downbeat reaction to a town that, at the time, was clearly sinking into the economic doldrums. 'It must be acknowledged', he declared, 'this very place is a surprise to a stranger, and especially one whose business is observation, as mine was.'

Defoe could hardly have been expected to know that better times were on the horizon for Kirkcudbright, and that when Lord Cockburn visited the town in 1844, that most distinguished Criminal Judge would be able to record in his book *Circuit Journeys*: 'I doubt if there can be a more picturesque country town in Scotland. Small, clean, silent and respectable it seems the type of place to which decent characters and moderate purses would retire for quiet comfort.' In fact, he was so impressed by what he found that he dubbed Kirkcudbright the 'Venice of Scotland'.

❧ ❧ ❧

Present-day Kirkcudbright remains a picturesque small town, set on the estuary of the River Dee at the edge of the Solway Firth: a coastal resort with its own working harbour and fleet of sea-going trawlers. There is a great deal to interest the present-day tourist, many of whom can be found during the balmy days of the summer months sauntering among the congeries of attractive streets and closes that grace the heart of the old town, with many of the houses attractively painted and decked out with luxuriant window-boxes and lustrous hanging baskets, thus adding yet more colour to the overall effect.

The seventeenth-century Tolbooth, which once served – among other things – as the local prison but is now an Art Centre, and the remains of the late-sixteenth-century MacLellan's Castle are foremost among Kirkcudbright's great historical attractions. Meanwhile, on a literary note it is inevitable that Kirkcudbright, in common with almost every town in the region, should have a connection with Robert Burns. Excise duties brought him to the place, where he stayed at the eighteenth-century Heid Inn (now called the 'Selkirk Arms') in the High Street. He also visited the town, and lodged at the same hostelry, during his first Galloway tour of 1793.

However, for anyone who is interested in Kirkcudbright's artistic heritage and the important role it plays in the history of the town, the eighteenth-century Broughton House situated in the High Street is an essential port of call. Originally built as the town residence for the Murrays of Broughton, the property became the home in 1901 of the artist Edward Atkinson Hornel, who might perhaps be aptly described as the presiding genius – and certainly the most prominent and widely successful member – of Kirkcudbright's artistic community during the early years of the twentieth century. Writing about him in his book *Some Dumfries and Galloway Men* (1922), in a piece originally published as an article in the *Dumfries and Galloway Standard*, James Reid declared, perhaps with an unconscious dash of hyperbole, that:

The Selkirk Arms, in the town's High Street.

No name is better known among art lovers all the world over than that of Mr E.A. Hornel, whose strong individualistic work has perhaps been the subject of greater controversy evoking more enthusiastic admiration on the one hand and more criticism on the other than that of any other modern painter ... The people of Kirkcudbright have every reason to be proud of the fact that Mr Hornel has not – as so many other Scottish artists have done – transferred his residence to the neighbourhood of London, but has remained faithful to the town of his upbringing and to the district which he loves and admires more than any other place on earth. He is in the fortunate position of not requiring to do so. Art collectors are only too glad to journey to Kirkcudbright when they know that a Hornel canvas is obtainable ...

Hornel was not a native of Kirkcudbright in the strictest sense of the word, but he was the next best thing to it. He was born in Australia, but came to Britain and was taken to Kirkcudbright in 1866 at the age of two, when his parents returned to live in the town after having emigrated to the other side of the world some years earlier. In fact, the Hornel family's connection with Kirkcudbright is said to extend as far back as the late sixteenth century. Reid noted that once Broughton House had served its time as the Murray family's town residence, 'it was the parish manse, and as such was frequently visited by Mr Hornel in his boyhood days. He then thought it a beautiful house which he should like to possess.'

Hornel studied art in Edinburgh and Antwerp and, more unusually perhaps, he later spent some considerable time living and painting in Japan. He belonged to a group of artists who became known as the 'Glasgow Boys', a coterie of predominantly

Broughton House was Hornel's home for more than thirty years.

like-minded artists which, as its name suggests, had close links with the city of Glasgow and came to public attention during the 1880s before petering out in the early years of the twentieth century. The group included, among others, James Guthrie (who was subsequently knighted) and Hornel's close friend, Ayrshire-born George Henry.

Broughton House, which Hornel was able to purchase when he was at the height of his fame, remained his home until his death in 1933. Following the death in 1950 of his sister Tizzy, who had lived with him and, as Reid phrased it, presided over the house with 'gracious hospitality', the property and its contents were left in trust, to be enjoyed by the people of Kirkcudbright and visitors to the Stewartry.

Hornel's visit to Japan in 1893 (which he had undertaken in the company of George Henry), and other trips to Ceylon and Burma, not only had an important effect on the style and nature of his subsequent work as an artist, but also influenced the development of the magnificent garden that he created – and which is now restored to its full glory – at the rear of his home. No visit to Broughton House would be complete without taking the opportunity to stroll along the garden's narrow paths and secluded avenues, while stopping occasionally to admire some of the rare and exotic plants and shrubs that flourish in the well-tended flower-beds along the way. (Anyone who has ever attended a concert in the Gallery at Broughton House, during the annual early summer Dumfries and Galloway Arts Festival, and chosen to enjoy their interval glass of wine in the garden, will know for themselves what a delightful spot it is.)

Meanwhile, inside Broughton House much of the decoration and furnishings would be instantly familiar to Hornel were he able to return today. The house was re-opened to the public in April 2005 after a period of closure, following the award of £1 million from the Heritage Lottery Fund. This huge injection of money allowed the National Trust for Scotland, which has owned the property since 1997, to implement a wide-ranging conservation project. Broughton House can boast not only an important selection of Hornel's own paintings – some of them, such as 'Girls Picking Blue Flax' (1917), which hangs in the gallery, inspired by and depicting local subjects – but also examples of work by various other artists who were drawn to Kirkcudbright and the surrounding area by Hornel's presence there, including W.S. MacGeorge and Bessie MacNicol.

In its heyday, during the late-1890s and much of the first half of the twentieth century, the artistic community that descended on Kirkcudbright and its environs was inevitably of a diverse kind, embracing – as Dorothy L. Sayers described in the extract from *Five Red Herrings* quoted at the beginning of this chapter – practitioners in a wide range of different mediums, and with some of its members undoubtedly achieving greater recognition and more enduring reputations than others. However, the Kirkcudbright 'colony', as it is often referred to, was in no sense a static entity; it comprised some people who settled in and around the town, liked what they found and stayed for the rest of their lives. Others came for weeks or months at a time, either returning repeatedly over the course of years or not, as the case may be. By no means were all of those artists, whom we look back upon as members of this diverse group, present at the same time.

Among some of the most prominent names to crop up in this ever-shifting community were William Mouncey, the already-mentioned George Henry, Charles Oppenheimer and Jessie M. King. Mouncey, in fact, was a genuinely local man; a Kirkcudbright native born in 1852 who, in the fullness of time, followed in his father's footsteps and became a decorator and house painter. He rarely ventured far away from the town and, three years after his death in 1901, at the early age of forty-nine (by which time he had married Hornel's sister, Margaret), Malcolm Harper, who was a local friend of Mouncey's, wrote admiringly in the *Gallovidian* of the man who only became a professional artist quite late in his life:

> Mouncey … like all true landscape painters … did not require to roam far afield for subjects. Well pleased was he always with the natural beauties of the surroundings of his home, from which he drew inspiration for the creation of his … works. Thus he was cradled and brought up in the midst of the scenery in which he delighted.

George Henry was drawn to the area by Hornel during the mid-1880s, and painted one of his most notable local scenes, *A Galloway Landscape,* in 1889. The two men collaborated on some of their work at one time: 'The Druids Bringing in the Mistletoe' (1890) and 'The Star in the East' (1891) are two examples of this slightly unusual

One of the delightful closes in the heart of old Kirkcudbright.

method of working. Later, their friendship waned and Henry subsequently moved to London, where he died during the Second World War.

Manchester-born Charles Oppenheimer moved to Kirkcudbright in 1908 when he was in his early thirties, and lived at first in the High Street next door to Hornel. By this time, he had studied at Manchester School of Art and in Italy. Once he had settled in he spent the rest of his life in Kirkcudbright, serving his local community as a Special Constable and also becoming a member of the town council. By the time he died in 1961, he had produced many fine paintings that were inspired by his adopted local surroundings, including 'Kirkcudbright Under Snow', 'Ebb Tide, Kirkcudbright' and 'From a Tower, Kirkcudbright'.

Jessie Marion King, a painter and children's book illustrator, was born in Glasgow in 1875, and studied at the city's School of Art, before living in Lancashire and Paris with her husband E.A. Taylor, whose own diverse talents embraced not only painting but also work in stained glass and furniture design. They arrived in Kirkcudbright during the First World War and – like Oppenheimer – remained living and working in the town for the rest of their days. (King died in 1949 and Taylor two years later.) Anyone seeking a comprehensive and frequently entertaining account of the many different artists who gravitated to and around Kirkcudbright over the years need look no further than Haig Gordon's absorbing *Tales of the Kirkcudbright Artists* (2006), from which few – if any – of the personalities who made their mark on the place have been omitted.

The Greengate in the High Street, where Jessie King and her husband lived.

In a fascinating postscript to its long history and still enduring reputation as the 'Artists' Town', it is interesting to note that Kirkcudbright had its own part to play in the early 1970s' cult horror film *The Wicker Man*. Starring Edward Woodward and the doyen of that genre, Christopher Lee, the action of this sometimes chilling film, which has steadily gained in status and popularity over the years, is set on a remote Scottish island; a fact which did not deter the makers of the film from shooting some of the street scenes in Kirkcudbright. More than one fan of *The Wicker Man* has been drawn to the town to view for themselves the locations that were employed in the production.

In its turn, the title of the film lives on in the name of the increasingly popular Wickerman Festival which, since 2002, has been held at the height of each summer on farmland a few miles east of Kirkcudbright. Spreading itself over more than 100 acres, the Wickerman is believed to be Scotland's largest 'alternative' festival. One undeniable highlight of the two-day event, amidst the music and other myriad diversions, is the late-night burning of a huge Wicker Man – all of which is a far cry from Daniel Defoe's day, when he noted of Kirkcudbright and its surroundings that '… they have no assemblies here, or balls.'

NINE

DEATH BY THE DEVIL'S BEEF TUB

> There's death tonight in the whirling snow
> That drifts through Annandale,
> But leal are the hearts of the men who go
> With the Edinboro' Mail.

Few visitors to the small and congested churchyard in Moffat will be familiar with these lines by the nineteenth-century poet, John Kelso Kelly. However, if they should happen to linger for a few moments among the oppressively tall gravestones, and read the inscriptions carved on two red sandstone memorials raised by public subscription in 1835, they will be told the same melancholy tale by each of them. One of the memorials is 'sacred to the memory of James MacGeorge, Guard of the Dumfries and Edinburgh Royal Mail, who unfortunately perished … after the most strenuous exertions in the performance of his duty.' The other is 'in memory of John Goodfellow, Driver, who perished on Erick Stane [*sic*] … in kindly assisting his fellow sufferer, the Guard, to carry forward the Mail Bags.' Together, these memorials represent the final scene in a drama played out near the Devil's Beef Tub, four miles or so north of Moffat, on 1 February 1831.

The first mail-coach route in Scotland had been introduced less than half a century earlier, in 1786. Prior to that, according to John Palmer who is credited with introducing the service:

> The mails are generally entrusted to some idle boy, without character, mounted on a worn-out hack, and who, so far from being able to defend himself or escape from a robber, is much more likely to be in league with him … The Post, at present, instead of being the swiftest, is almost the slowest conveyance in the country; and though, from the improvements in our roads, other carriers have proportionately mended their speed, the Post is as slow as ever.

❦ ❦ ❦

Headstones in Moffat churchyard, in memory of Goodfellow and MacGeorge.

Today, the A701 road from Dumfries to Edinburgh meanders through some of the most dramatic and beautiful scenery that southern Scotland has to offer, and more or less follows the same course as the old coaching route of the mid-nineteenth century. One of the most spectacular natural features along this journey of more than seventy miles is undoubtedly the Devil's Beef Tub, a great hollow in the hills whose rim is skirted by the main road after it has swept around the windy heights of Ericstane Brae, and climbed 1,000ft in its ascent from Moffat.

The steep-sided Beef Tub is formed by three hills, two of which are over 1,500ft in height. 'A deep, black, blackguard-looking abyss of a hole it is,' wrote Sir Walter Scott in *Redgauntlet*, 'and goes straight down from the roadside as perpendicular as it can.' The description is as accurate today as ever it was, and it is easy to understand how this immense cauldron – over 600ft deep, and half a mile across at the top – was once such a popular hiding-place for stolen cattle.

Nowadays, the summit of this vast, natural amphitheatre is easily reached by car, a mere ten minutes' drive north from the old spa resort of Moffat. It is a fair climb, nevertheless, with a rise of 815ft up Ericstane Brae over a distance of less than two miles. In 1831, when the coaching route between Dumfries and Edinburgh was divided into eight stages, the third stage (of seven miles) – from Moffat, up Ericstane and past the Beef Tub to the inn at Tweedshaws – was reckoned to be one of the most arduous that Scottish coaching services had to endure. Leslie Gardiner, writing in his

The deep hollow of the Devil's Beef Tub.

book *Stage Coach to John O' Groats* (1961), recalled the experience of a traveller during the 1820s 'who encountered one load of passengers on the Moffat hills in midwinter who were screaming and moaning most pathetically, for no other reason than that the sight of the desolate moor they had to cross had sent them all into hysterics.'

A passenger on the Dumfries to Edinburgh Mail, Will Caesar, wrote a jolly poem about his experience of the journey; the verses give no hint of the dangers and hardships that such an expedition could involve:

> I took the mail on Tuesday's morn,
> A blyther man was never born;
> The horse were fleet – weel fed wi' corn –
> We scoured away;
> The guard employed his bugle horn
> Right oft that day.

We got fresh horse at Bourance Rig,
Were soon in view o' Saint Ann's brig,
And saw Raehills, sae braw and trig,
Stand up the glen;
And mony a tree and bonny twig
Adorn the fen.

We hied us on to Moffat town,
Saw Annan Water rennin' down,
And Granton standing up aboun
Near the Beef-tub,
Named for the devil, filthy loun,
Vile Beelzebub.

Had Caesar been travelling on that same route on Tuesday 1 February 1831, he would have had a dark tale indeed to tell. Stories of coaching accidents, of course, were by no means uncommon, with winter and rough weather contributing to a greater share than was usual throughout the rest of the year. Gardiner recorded a number of such incidents, culled from the pages of contemporary newspaper reports and official documents. One such account concerns a disaster that occurred in 1808 at Elvanfoot, not many miles across the hills from the Devil's Beef Tub. 'Up and down mails [from the south to Glasgow] met at Elvanfoot,' Gardiner explained, but on this occasion 'the road collapsed and the up coach, first on the scene, fell into the storm-swollen Evan Water. Three horses and two passengers were drowned, coachman, guard and everyone else seriously injured …' An incident reminiscent of that which forms the subject of this chapter befell the Brighton to London Mail in the 1820s, when 'eight miles from Brighton it fell into a drift from which it was impossible to extricate itself without further assistance.' Having left Brighton on Sunday, '… the guard did not reach town until 7 o'clock on Tuesday night', the news report informed its readers, 'having been obliged to travel with the mail-bags on horse-back and in many instances to leave the main road and proceed across fields in order to avoid deep drifts of snow.'

Tuesday 1 February dawned in Dumfries with snow and strong winds. In fact, similar weather conditions had prevailed for more than a week and, according to Gardiner, writing in 1961, 'for three dark months in 1831 the whole of the north was snowbound. Aged residents in Kilmarnock recall grandfathers' tales of Glasgow coaches buried deep on Fenwick Moor, with passengers huddling inside, wrapped up in straw like so many outsize wine bottles. Search parties walked on top of them and, having located them, could do no more than dig a chimney in the snow to get air to the vehicles and their horses.'

However, despite the appalling weather conditions, the Edinburgh Mail – the coach was appropriately named *Hero* – set off as usual from the post office in Dumfries

The Balmoral, Moffat, was formerly the Spur Inn.

(accounts of the departure time vary between 7 a.m. and 10.30 a.m.), carrying on this occasion two female passengers inside the vehicle. The reins of the four horses were in the eminently capable hands of John Goodfellow, described as 6ft tall, strongly built and approaching fifty years of age. The mail bags were in the care of the forty-seven year-old guard, James MacGeorge, 'of ruddy complexion and inflexible will'. The two men had been working together on the same route for ten years, and were a highly experienced crew.

The first twenty-one miles or so from Dumfries, over gently undulating terrain, were uneventful but hard going nevertheless. As *Hero* travelled north out of Dumfries and through Amisfield to the first stage at Burrance, then on by way of St Ann's and Beattock, it was increasingly hampered by driving snow. As a result, when Goodfellow and MacGeorge pulled up to change horses at the second stage, the Spur Inn, Moffat (now the Balmoral Hotel), it was already 2 p.m. Mr Cranstoun, landlord of the Spur, implored the guard and driver to postpone their journey until the next day. It was already growing dark, even though the afternoon was still quite young, and the blizzard raging in Moffat's wide High Street was sufficient proof – were any needed – of the wild and hazardous conditions they were bound to encounter on the steep and winding road up to the Devil's Beef Tub. However, neither Goodfellow (himself a Moffat man) nor MacGeorge could be persuaded to delay their departure overnight. 'They quarrelled me once,' said the guard, referring to a previous storm some years earlier, when he had stopped short at Moffat, only to be reprimanded by his employers. 'They'll not quarrel me this time.' He could not have imagined the deadly accuracy of his prophecy. There is no doubt that the GPO at that time could prove a hard taskmaster, as this circular letter from GPO Headquarters, dated November 1804, quoted in Edmund Vale's *The Mail-Coach Men of the Late-Eighteenth Century* (1960), and addressed to all Mail Guards, amply demonstrates.

> Mail Guards are fully apprised of their Duty by every Direction and Instruction given them … [the capital letters are the GPO's]; they are also fully informed of the punishment that must overtake them, if they are found out in breaking or neglecting it; but so many Guards have of late, in defiance of every Admonition, been guilty of great Misconduct, that it has been determined on to dismiss some, fully hoping that such a Step will act as an Example to the Remainder; but should it not, for any Breach of their instructions they will be dismissed.

There followed a list of guards who were to be made an example of, including 'COX: for having taken up a parcel at Bristol to deliver at Tetbury … which Parcel was found in his Mail Box', and 'FAGAN: for carrying fish and not paying the carriage …' It is no wonder, then, that MacGeorge felt impelled to press on with the journey to Edinburgh, despite the atrocious weather, rather than incur the wrath of his employers and even possibly lose his job.

❧ ❧ ❧

Two extra horses were taken on at the Spur Inn, making a total of six in all and, just after 4 p.m. *Hero*, with the customary blast from MacGeorge's bugle, set off into the storm and the quickly fading daylight. The two ladies from Dumfries also elected to continue their journey and from this point onwards the coach was also accompanied by the Moffat road mender, James Marchbank who, it was decided, could be sent back to the Spur to obtain assistance in the event of any mishap.

As *Hero* left Moffat and struck out into open country beyond, the force of the blizzard increased considerably and, only two miles from the village, at Gardenholm, the Dumfries and Edinburgh Mail became embedded in a deep snow-drift, from which not even the strength of six powerful horses could liberate it. The horses were unharnessed without delay, and four of them were sent back to Moffat in the care of James Marchbank, but not before the road mender had tried once more – and, again, in vain – to persuade Goodfellow and MacGeorge to abandon their journey for that night. A few hours later Marchbank, accompanied by Mr Cranstoun, reached *Hero* with a post chaise. Together, they managed to convey the two ladies – one of whom, by now, was almost unconscious with the cold – back to the warmth of a roaring fire and a hot meal at the Spur.

In the meantime, Goodfellow and MacGeorge, taking one of the two remaining horses each, had begun to make their way with the leather mail bags intending to reach the next stage along the route, which was the inn at Tweedshaws. However, there were five arduous miles to be covered between the stranded *Hero* and their destination, and their progress must have been desperately slow as they followed the steep and meandering road up Ericstane Brae in blizzard conditions. (Regular travellers making the same journey today – although the course of the road is somewhat altered – will

Lonely Corehead.

know how quickly this route can become impassable at the Devil's Beef Tub during winter snowstorms.)

After covering about three miles, the men abandoned their horses. The poor creatures were either simply exhausted or otherwise quite unable to make any further headway in the deep snow. Somehow, later that same night, they turned up without their rides down at Corehead Farm – the first house in the steep-sided valley issuing out of the Beef Tub – far below.

In the meantime, it would appear that Goodfellow and MacGeorge had divided the mail bags between them and continued on foot along the road skirting the summit bearing, it is believed, well in excess of 50lbs each. They were carrying no lantern with them, and so it must have proved almost impossible to see their way ahead in the darkness as they struggled through deep snowdrifts, their strength rapidly dwindling. At the sixth snow-post from Moffat – these were placed at intervals of a mile in this wild country, to help guide travellers in blizzard conditions – they put down their bags, tying them around the post for safety's sake, with fingers that were by now bleeding badly from frostbite. A report in the *Dumfries and Galloway Courier* stated that:

> [Goodfellow and MacGeorge], when they arrived at the snow-post, must have been perfectly collected, from the pains they took, not only to exhibit the mail bags, but to prevent the wind from blowing them away … This last heroic action of their lives equals in devotion the conduct of the wounded ensign, who wraps the colours round his body to prevent them falling into the hands of the enemy …

The isolated stretch of road leading to the sixth snow-post.

The following day, when the blizzard conditions had somewhat abated, and in the wake of the general alarm occasioned by the appearance of the riderless horses at Corehead, James Marchbank set out from Moffat in search of the guard and driver. Making his way past the abandoned *Hero*, by now almost completely hidden in the snow at Gardenholm, he toiled alone up Ericstane Brae and over the Beef Tub. He found the mail bags, where they had been tied to the sixth snow-post but, except for the dark stains left by their bleeding fingers, there was no sign of the two men. All around was the profound silence which follows a heavy fall of snow; a blanket of white stretching from the tops of the Lowther and Tweedsmuir Hills down into the most distant reaches of Annandale. The day closed in, forcing Marchbank's return to Moffat before he could reach the inn at Tweedshaws, to establish whether or not Goodfellow and MacGeorge had arrived there safely.

On Thursday, after the landlord of the inn at Tweedshaws had confirmed that neither of the two men had passed that way, it was decided that, as the snowstorms had eased, a search-party should be organised without further delay to particularly comb the area around the sixth snow-post. The *Dumfries and Galloway Courier* reported that:

> The anxiety of the people of Moffat was now extreme and the only individual who behaved ill was the Town Crier, who refused to sound the tocsin for a general muster until he knew who was to reward him for his trouble! Notwithstanding of this, a numerous party, consisting of nearly 150 persons, immediately left the village determined to search everywhere for the unfortunate men. Some were armed with poles, and others

The monument erected in memory of the two men who perished at this spot in 1831.

with spades, and though they continued to search till fairly spent, all they discovered was the driver's hat, which was found in a moss adjoining the snow-post.

It was not until Saturday, four days after they had set off from their stranded vehicle, that the bodies of John Goodfellow and James MacGeorge were eventually found in deep snow by a further search-party, 'when about half a mile beyond the snow-post, they observed the points of a man's shoes sticking through the snow', continued the *Dumfries and Galloway Courier* report:

> … and discovered John Goodfellow stretched on his back … his death-bed colder than the grave itself. On looking around they observed something black, and about a hundred yards further came upon the remains of James MacGeorge, half erect, and in the attitude of sleep … Those who had struggled so manfully for life and duty were in their dying moments not far divided; it is even conjectured that MacGeorge watched by his friend till he expired, and then made a last and desperate effort to preserve his own valuable life.

On 9 February, after the weather had improved sufficiently for the two bodies to be carried down to Moffat, Goodfellow and MacGeorge were laid to rest in the village churchyard. It was reported in the following week's edition of the *Dumfries and Galloway Courier* that '… the inhabitants of the surrounding country assumed on the occasion the character of one great family of mourners.'

In 1931, to mark the 100th anniversary of the tragic event, a simple stone cairn was placed by the roadside on the site of the sixth snow-post, where it can be seen today; a permanent reminder of the courage and devotion to duty displayed by two brave men. A panel set into the cairn bears a carved replica of the guard's bugle and an inscription to the memory of Goodfellow and MacGeorge who, it states, 'On 1st February 1831 … lost their lives in the snow after carrying the bags thus far.'

❧ ❧ ❧

Within just a few decades of the tragedy that overtook Goodfellow and MacGeorge, the mail-coach would become redundant, consigned to the past by the development of the railways. In the meantime, however, those men charged with the duty of carrying the mail between Dumfries and Edinburgh continued to encounter serious danger along the way especially, as always, during the winter months. A guard on the Edinburgh Mail in January 1839, for example, reported of his journey that:

> The snow began to fall as he left Moffat, and continued all the way to Edinburgh – within five miles of which it was so deep that the mail [coach] had to be dug out. On [his] return he had to leave the road at the same place, but with the assistance of additional leaders they reached Broughton … The night was truly gloomy and the storm appalling.

On this occasion, the guard was fortunate and lived to tell the tale – unlike Goodfellow and MacGeorge, whose deaths on the lonely snowbound road beyond the Devil's Beef Tub eclipsed all other mishaps on the mail-coach route between Dumfries and Edinburgh.

☙ TEN ☙

QUINTINSHILL AND THE DEVIL'S PORRIDGE

Many thousands of people pass through lonely Quintinshill, near Gretna, every day of the week on that stretch of the main west coast railway line that runs between Carlisle and Lockerbie. Perhaps some of these travellers, engrossed in their laptops or newspapers, may lift their heads for a moment to survey the flat landscape of the coastal plain, which forms the main setting on this part of their journey close to the Solway Firth. However, few of them will be aware that, while being transported so swiftly to their various destinations, at Quintinshill they are passing the scene of a terrible accident that even today, not far short of a century later, still bears the unenviable distinction of being Britain's worst railway disaster. The calamity, that occurred less than a year after the outbreak of the First World War, was rendered even more poignant owing to the fact that, out of the 227 passengers and railway crew who were killed on that occasion (a further 246 people were injured), 214 of the fatalities were sustained by men of the 1/7th(Leith) Battalion of the Royal Scots who, after months of intensive training and keen anticipation, were *en route* from Larbert in Stirlingshire to Liverpool, from where they were due to sail on the *Empress of India* to take part in the Gallipoli Campaign.

The sequence of events which culminated in this appalling tragedy unfolded in the early morning of Saturday 22 May 1915, on what proved to be – according to eye-witness accounts at the time – a fine and increasingly hot late spring day. The bare facts of the case were reported in the pages of the *Dumfries and Galloway Standard*:

> Three trains were involved in the disaster … one of them carrying about 550 officers and men of the 7th Royal Scots … The scene of the accident was Quintinshill siding, which is half a mile north of Gretna station. The military train dashed into a local passenger train which was standing on the same line, opposite the signal box, and the overturned carriages fouled the other main line. Almost at the same moment a London express travelling at a high speed, and drawn by two powerful locomotives, ploughed into the wreckage. The shattering horror of the collision was followed by an outbreak of fire,

The stretch of railway line at Quintinshill today.

exacting a toll of life and suffering unprecedented in the annals of British railways … The scenes which followed beggar description … After the dreadful crash had shattered the restful quiet of the surrounding district … there was a sudden hush as if Nature herself stood aghast at the hideous spectacle. Then all was chaos and confusion … There was a medley of horrible sounds that the worst delirium could not equal. In the midst of the wreckage were four great engines broken and twisted as if by some giant hand. From one of them, propelled by some unseen force, came huge pieces of metal, which were sent high into the air and fell to earth with great violence rendering rescue work in the vicinity impossible.

A vivid eye-witness account of the immediate aftermath of the crash was gathered by the *Standard*'s reporter from a local man, Mr Andrew Sword, who lived about half a mile away from the dreadful scene and who was at work in a field when he heard the sound of the first impact. 'I looked across quickly, and saw two trains had crashed into each other:

'Good Lord!, I said to myself, 'is that the express?' for it was overdue. But, looking to the left towards Gretna, I saw the express travelling at the top of its speed across Quintinshill Bridge. The two colliding trains [the troop train and the local passenger service] shot into flame. The express [travelling north from London] rushed on. The signalman could never stop it. I was paralysed. Like a flash it was into the other two; dug into the middle of them and raised a hill of wreckage. The flames spouted out of the wreckage higher and higher. There were bursts as if something were exploding … With a great effort I moved and ran across the fields to the wreck. I found speed as I moved, and raced across the fields like mad … I was the second one on the scene …

Undoubtedly, the death-toll would have been even higher had not the driver of the London to Glasgow express been able to slow down his train at the last moment. A passenger travelling from London was reported in the *Standard* as saying that:

> … the train was going at about thirty-five miles an hour in approaching Quintinshill [somewhat slower, it would seem, than the impression gained by Mr Sword] but, thanks to the smartness of the driver in applying the brakes, that speed was very much reduced before the other wrecked trains were reached. The train was slowed down to such an extent that the impact was but slightly felt in the middle and rear carriages of the train.

It is impossible to calculate on what scale lives would have been lost and injuries sustained in the accident had not fire subsequently ripped through the wreckage, but the flames themselves obviously claimed many additional lives and inflicted further injury to a considerable number of those casualties who ultimately survived the horrors of that day. A lethal concoction of elderly wooden carriages (of which the troop train was mainly comprised), together with ammunition being carried on board, and gas oil lamps to provide the lighting, is generally thought to be the most likely cause of the all-consuming fire that raged and smouldered as rescuers picked their way through the terrible scene of destruction.

In order to understand the reasons for the accident happening at all, it is necessary to look at what took place inside the Quintinshill signal box during the early hours of that Saturday morning. Two railway signalmen who were on duty there were subsequently charged with causing the fatal accident as a result of the disastrous errors they had made.

Lord Strathclyde presided over the legal proceedings at the High Court in Edinburgh and John Thomas, in his book (published in 1969) *Gretna: Britain's Worst Railway Disaster (1915)*, has quoted from his summary of the sequence of events, delivered for the benefit of the jury:

> At 6.43 on the morning of the day in question the men in the signal box at Quintinshill were asked to accept the troop train coming from the north. They accepted it. That meant that they gave a signal to the north that the line was clear and that the troop train might safely come on. At that very moment when the signal was given there was before the very eyes of the men in the signal box a local train which was obstructing the line on which the troop train was to run. One man in the signal box had actually left that train a few minutes before, just at the time when it was being shunted on to the up line. The other man had a few minutes before directed the local train to leave the down main and go on to the up main. That is the staggering fact that confronts you …

The Quintinshill memorial in Rosebank cemetery, Leith.

Quintinshill memorial at the rear of the Old Blacksmith's Shop, Gretna Green, just a short distance from the site of the railway disaster.

Both signalmen were subsequently found guilty of culpable homicide, and each of them served a custodial sentence. A third employee, a railway fireman, was found not guilty of the charges laid against him.

As with those railway passengers who speed through Quintinshill today, unaware of the significance of the spot they are passing, probably only a handful of Edinburgh's many visitors each year will make their way a short distance from the city centre to the quiet corner of Rosebank cemetery in Leith where the remains of 214 members of the 1/7th (Leith) Battalion of the Royal Scots were laid to rest, shortly after the accident in which they perished. A granite memorial, in the form of an Ionian Cross (behind which stands a wall bearing ten tablets filled with the names of all those who died), was unveiled by Lord Rosebery (the regiment's Honorary Colonel) during a ceremony conducted in May 1916, a year after the crash, and it can still be seen today. 'For long years to come we shall be haunted by the shock of the trains, and the groans of the dying,' declared Lord Rosebery, 'for long years to come we shall seem to see the freshness of that summer morning blurred by the anguish and agony of the catastrophe ... and for generations men and women will come to visit this cross.'

However, much closer to the scene of the accident, on the edge of an exposed car park situated behind the world-famous Old Blacksmith's Shop at Gretna Green (and from where the site of the crash can be glimpsed), another memorial – in the form of a low stone cairn – can be found. It is surmounted by a plaque, which reminds us that civilian passengers and railway employees also perished in the Gretna disaster. The memorial was unveiled on the eightieth anniversary, in May 1995, and the ceremony was performed by a Mrs R. Buchanan who, as a very young girl, had survived the crash in which, tragically, her mother and brother lost their lives.

As the ill-fated troop train hurtled down the line towards Quintinshill, it would shortly have passed close to the site – had not the crash intervened – earmarked for what would become over the following months HM Factory Gretna. This vast munitions works, which covered nearly ten miles by the time it was completed, reached from Longtown, just across the border with England, to Dornock near Annan. Although it was built on an unprecedented scale, there was – for obvious security reasons, given the sensitive nature of its purpose in those dark days of the First World War – no evidence of the factory's existence to be found on the local Ordnance Survey maps. The two townships (as they were known) of Gretna and Eastriggs were created to house people who came to the area to work at this huge industrial complex ranged along the northern edge of the Solway, in what had hitherto been very sparsely populated country.

Sir Arthur Conan Doyle, the world-famous creator of the amateur sleuth, Sherlock Holmes, paid a visit to HM Factory Gretna towards the end of 1916 and, in an article which subsequently appeared in the *Annandale Observer*, he recorded his impressions of what he found there:

> One of the miracles of present day Britain is a place which we will call Moorside [the codename employed by the authorities to disguise the existence of the munitions plant]. Perhaps it is the most remarkable place in the world. Only a little more than a year ago, say September 1915, it was a lonely peat bog fringing the sea, with a hinterland of desolate plain, over which the gulls swooped and screamed. Then the great hand of the Minister of Munitions was stretched out to this lonely and inhospitable waste, for it chanced to lie with good rail and water connections and not too remote from centres of coal and of iron.

The isolated and sequestered nature of the area, some distance from any large centre of population, made it the ideal spot in which to build a factory that was to produce the explosive material cordite on a grand scale, with output of the substance eventually climbing to 800 tons a week.

HM Factory Gretna was commissioned in direct response to the poorly-equipped British Army's urgent need for ammunition, and cordite was employed in the shells and bullets that were despatched to the Front. The cordite-making process itself was a

Above: *The Hunter's Lodge Hotel in Annan Road, Gretna, was a Staff Club in the days of HM Factory, Gretna.*

Below: *Central Avenue, Gretna, pictured today.*

laborious and, above all, an exceedingly dangerous one, and required the most stringent adherence to safety procedures on the part of the largely female workforce who were engaged in its manufacture, as Conan Doyle went on to explain, after visiting ...

> ... the wide buildings where the raw cotton is stored, where the crude glycerine is refined, where the ether and alcohol are distilled, and where finally the perfect gun-cotton is completed. Thence by little trains it is conveyed over yonder to that rising ground which is called Nitro-Glycerine Hill ... There the nitro-glycerine on the one side and the gun-cotton on the other are kneaded together into a sort of devil's porridge ... This, by the way, is where the danger comes in. The least generation of heat may cause an explosion. Those smiling khaki-clad girls who are swirling the stuff round in their hands would be blown to atoms in an instant if certain very small changes occurred.

The novelist, biographer and critic, Rebecca West, also visited the factory in 1916 in her capacity as a journalist, and heartily echoed Conan Doyle's observations about the thousands of women who were helping to produce the cordite, declaring that:

> ... they face more danger every day than any soldier on home defence has seen since the beginning of the war ... It is because of this army of cheerful and disciplined workers that this cordite factory has been able to increase its output since the beginning of the war by something over 1,500 per cent ... Surely never before in modern history can women have lived a life so completely parallel to that of the Regular Army. The girls who take up this work sacrifice almost as much as men who enlist; although they make on average 30s a week they are working much harder than most of them, particularly the large number who were formerly domestic servants, would ever have dreamed of working in peacetime.

❧ ❧ ❧

It is hard to overestimate the initial impact that the creation of HM Factory Gretna – sometimes described as 'the greatest factory on earth' – made upon that quiet land at the edge of the Solway, as hordes of navvies (up to 15,000 of them) descended on the place to undertake the extensive building work required before the plant could get underway. The influx of such large numbers of men, a great proportion of whom spent the best part of their free time drinking alcohol to excess, inevitably made a considerable impression – and a far from favourable one – in the locality. Being the nearest large centre of population, it was Carlisle that often bore the brunt of their unquenchable thirsts, and particularly so at the weekends.

Following the arrival of the navvies, convictions for drunkenness and drink-related offences in Carlisle and the surrounding area stood at just short of 1,000 in 1916, which represented a fourfold increase on previous recent statistics. Realising that urgent action must be taken to curb the problem, the Government set up a Central Control Board (Liquor Traffic), which effectively brought under state control all the breweries and public houses in the area. The implications of this unique measure (some aspects

St John's Church, Eastriggs, (above) was home to the Devil's Porridge exhibition for many years before it moved, in 2008, to this modern building at Daleside (below).

of which remained in place until the early 1970s) were far-reaching, but probably two of its most beneficial effects were to implement reduced levels of alcohol in the beer that was brewed and to restrict pub opening hours, with the result that an immediate improvement was recorded in alcohol-related convictions.

Once the navvies had constructed the factory buildings, a further 15,000 or so people poured into the area to work at the new plant. When operating at its full capacity, HM Factory Gretna's weekly output of cordite was said to be greater than that produced by all of Britain's other munitions works added together so, on that basis, its contribution to the national war effort can be judged a highly significant one. In the process, however, the workforce – of which approximately two-thirds were women – did not escape unharmed. Given the perilous nature of the work being undertaken, the number of fatalities was relatively low, although it should be noted that several hundred female munitions workers had perished nationwide by the end of the First World War. However, it was not unknown for employees to be temporarily overcome by poisonous fumes, for example, and no doubt the subsequent health of many workers at the Solway plant (and at munitions factories throughout the land) was permanently damaged by prolonged close contact with such toxic materials as went into the manufacture of the 'Devil's Porridge'.

Once the First World War had drawn to a close, the need for HM Factory Gretna evaporated and the plant was shut down. The munitions workers, many of whom had come from Britain's far-flung Empire overseas, dispersed to their homes, leaving the area relatively quiet again. Some of the land on which the factory had been built was acquired by the Ministry of Defence, who used it for the storage of ammunition and explosives. While nothing remains to be seen of the huge factory complex itself, beyond a few small remnants of the foundations and odd fragments of buildings, the townships of Eastriggs and Gretna remain as thriving and bustling communities to this day.

Our knowledge of day-to-day life at HM Factory Gretna and of its workforce would be considerably sketchier were it not for the existence of a remarkable exhibition which first opened its doors to the public during the summer of 1997 at St John's Church, Eastriggs, and which has since grown to become one of south-west Scotland's most popular tourist attractions. The appropriately named Devil's Porridge Exhibition (which continued to be housed at St John's every summer until 2007, after which it moved to Daleside, Eastriggs), not only provides the visitor with an unparalleled insight into the life of the former munitions plant itself, but also – through the aid of exhibitions, interactive experiences and special events – offers a broader perspective of life on the Home Front during both World Wars.

Bibliography

Chapter One

Crockett, W.S., *The Scott Originals* (Grant & Murray Ltd; Edinburgh, 1932 edn)

M'Diarmid, John, *Sketches from Nature* (Oliver & Boyd, Edinburgh/Simpkin & Marshall; London, 1830)

Scott, Sir Walter, *The Heart of Midlothian* (Oxford University Press World's Classics edn, ed. Claire Lamont, 1982)

Chapter Two

Bickford, Richard F., *The Story of John Paul Jones 1747-1792* (Tartan Edge, Dumfries, 1993)

de Koven, Mrs Reginald, *The Life and Letters of John Paul Jones* (Scribners, 1913)

Lockwood, David, *John Paul Jones – In Harm's Way* (Dumfries and Galloway Council Community Resources, Libraries, Arts and Museums, 1997)

Sherburne, John Henry, *The Life and Character of John Paul Jones* (1851)

Urquhart, James, *John Paul Jones 1776-1976. A Bicentennial Salute and Souvenir from Great Britain* (Sangspiel; Dumfries, 1981)

Vansittart, Peter, *John Paul Jones: A Restless Spirit* (Robson Books, 2004)

Chapter Three

Boyle, Andrew M., *The Ayrshire Book of Burns-Lore* (Alloway Publishing Ltd; Ayr, 1996 edn)

Davies, W.H. (ed.), *The Poetical Works of Burns* (Collins, Not Dated)

Lindsay, Maurice, *The Burns Encyclopaedia* (Robert Hale, 1980 edn)

Mackay, James A., *Burns-Lore of Dumfries and Galloway* (Alloway Publishing Ltd; Ayr, 1988)

Chapter Four

Dinwiddie, Revd John L., *The Ruthwell Cross and The Ruthwell Savings Bank* (Eighth edn, Solway Offset Services; Dumfries, 1999)

Duncan, Revd George John C., *Memoir of the Revd Henry Duncan D.D.* (William Oliphant & Sons; Edinburgh, 1848)

Chapter Five

Campbell, Ian, *Thomas Carlyle* (The Saltire Society edn.; Edinburgh, 1993)

Carlyle, Thomas, (Fielding, K.J., & Campbell, Ian, eds), *Reminiscences* (Oxford University Press, 1997)

Carlyle, Thomas, (Norton, Charles Eliot, ed.), *Reminiscences* (2 vols), (MacMillan & Co., 1887 edn)

Carlyle, Thomas, *Sartor Resartus* (Chapman & Hall edn, Not Dated)

Froude, J.A., *Life of Carlyle* (4 vols 1882 and 1884), (ed. Clubbe, John), (John Murray, 1979)

Holme, Thea, *The Carlyles at Home* (Oxford University Press, 1965)

Sloan, J.M., *The Carlyle Country* (Chapman & Hall, 1904)

Waugh, J.L., *Thornhill and its Worthies* (Thos. Hunter & Co.; Dumfries, 1913)

Chapter Six

Fairfoul's Guide to Moffat (Thos. M. Fairfoul, Moffat, 1879 edn.)

Gifford, John, *The Buildings of Scotland: Dumfries and Galloway* (Yale University Press edn, 2002)

Chapter Seven

All About Wanlockhead: A Brief History of Scotland's Highest Village (Wanlockhead Museum Trust, 1989)

Brown, James, *The History of Sanquhar* (J. Anderson & Son, Dumfries/John Menzies & Co.; Edinburgh and Glasgow, 1891)

Hastings, Revd Thomas, *A History of Wanlockhead* (written in 1862)

Houston, George, (ed.), *The Third Statistical Account of Scotland (The County of Dumfries)*, (Collins, Glasgow, 1962)

Porteous, Revd J. Moir, *God's Treasure-House in Scotland* (Simpkin, Marshall & Co., London/John Menzies & Co.; Edinburgh and Glasgow, 1876)

Wordsworth, Dorothy, *Recollections of a Tour Made in Scotland, AD 1803* (James Thin edn, Edinburgh, 1981)

Chapter Eight

Gordon, Haig, *Tales of the Kirkcudbright Artists* (Galloway Publishing, Kirkcudbright, 2006)

Reid, James, *Some Dumfries and Galloway Men* (Thos. Hunter, Watson & Co. Ltd, Dumfries, 1922)

Sayers, Dorothy L., *Five Red Herrings* (New English Library, Hodder & Stoughton, 2003 edn)

Somerville, Christopher, *Twelve Literary Walks* (W.H. Allen & Co., 1985)

Chapter Nine

Anon, Article in winter 1907 edn of the *Gallovidian*, reprinted from the *Dumfries and Galloway Courier* (February, 1831)

Corrie, John M., *The Dumfries Post Office 1642-1910* (The Council of the Dumfriesshire and Galloway Natural History and Antiquarian Society, Dumfries and Maxwelltown Ewart Public Library, 1912)

Gardiner, Leslie, *Stage Coach to John o' Groats* (Hollis & Carter, London, 1961)

Henderson, Thomas, *Moffat Early Roads and Coaching Days* (Annandale Observer Press, Annan, 1960)

Vale, Edmund, *The Mail-Coach Men of the Late-Eighteenth Century* (Cassell & Co., London 1960)

Chapter Ten

Anon, Reports in the *Dumfries and Galloway Standard* May 1915

Anon, *Quintinshill Rail Disaster* (A written memorial, commissioned by the Scottish Area of the Western Front Association. Not Dated)

Conan Doyle, Sir Arthur, *Eastriggs and Gretna – The Miracle Towns* (article in *Annandale Observer*, December 1916)

Routledge, Gordon L., *Gretna's Secret War* (Bookcase, Carlisle, 1999)

Thomas, John, *Gretna: Britain's Worst Railway Disaster (1915)* (David & Charles, Newton Abbot, 1969)

West, Rebecca, *The Cordite Makers* (article published in 1916)